THE UNFOLDING DRAMA

OF THE BIBLE

Drama of the Bible

EIGHT STUDIES INTRODUCING
THE BIBLE AS A WHOLE

Bernhard W. Anderson

PROFESSOR OF OLD TESTAMENT THEOLOGY
PRINCETON THEOLOGICAL SEMINARY

ASSOCIATION PRESS
NEW YORK

THE UNFOLDING DRAMA OF THE BIBLE

Copyright © 1971, 1957 by
National Board of Young Men's Christian Associations

Associa   291 Broadway, New York, N. Y. 10007

9-87

Standard Book Number: 8096–1815–X
Library of Congress catalog card number: 78–141870

Biblical quotations are from *The Revised Standard Version of the Bible and the Apochrypha.*

Second Printing, 1974

Printed in the United States of America

PREFACE TO THE SECOND EDITION

This Study Guide, which aims to help the reader to understand the full sweep of the Bible from beginning to end, was originally prepared for the 1952 Religion in Life program at Bucknell University, sponsored by the Christian Association. To the surprise of many, including the author, it proved to have a wide appeal, far beyond the original circle for whom it was intended. With the encouragement of leaders of the student movement, this Bucknell Study Guide was issued in revised form as a Haddam House Book in 1953 and later was reprinted with only slight changes as a Reflection Book in 1957.

It is with some reluctance that I have undertaken a revision of this Study Guide after almost two decades. My policy has been to retain the basic outline and much of the text of the original version. In some instances, however, I have proposed other biblical passages for study and I have added some new accents to the discussion for the sake of making the Study Guide more timely. Moreover, at the end of each study unit I have directed the reader to further literature, including my book *Rediscovering the Bible* (Association Press, 1951) and my more recent *Creation versus Chaos* (Association Press, 1967).

Admittedly, "the times they are a-changin'," to quote a folk-rock song. Nevertheless, the study of the Bible is not a passing fad but remains the vital source of a valid understanding of the Christian faith. It is my hope that this Study Guide may direct the reader into the Bible itself so that he may sense his involvement in what Amos Wilder calls "the great story and plot of all time and space" and that he may experience his relation to "the Great Dramatist . . . God himself."

BERNHARD W. ANDERSON
Princeton Theological Seminary
August 21, 1970

INTRODUCING THE BIBLE STUDY

In one of his well-known sonnets John Keats tells how in reading Chapman's translation of Homer he experienced the elation of a new discovery.

> Then felt I like some watcher of the skies
> When a new planet swims into his ken;
> Or, like stout Cortez, when with eagle eyes
> He stared at the Pacific—and all his men
> Looked at each other with a wild surmise—
> Silent, upon a peak in Darien.

In our time many have had a similar experience in reading the Bible. Bible Study, of the kind you are about to engage in, can have the result of opening your eyes to a startling new vista, of giving you a new perspective upon the meaning of your life and your place in the whole historical drama.

There are two ways to study the Bible. The first is appropriate to classroom or academic study. Using this approach, one *looks at* the Bible from the outside as a spectator. He learns many interesting things about the Bible, such as the literary process which brought it to its final shape as a canon of sacred Scripture, or the cultural, archaeological and historical background of the various books. He is curious about the ideas of the Bible, even the "idea of God," and perhaps he masters these ideas well enough to pass the course with flying colors. This descriptive approach has its place, but it is not the one we shall follow in these studies.

The second approach is one in which together we shall attempt to *stand within* the Bible and to look out at the world through the window of biblical faith. Like actors who put themselves into the script of a play, we shall read the Bible with personal involvement, realizing that it is not a textbook but "a letter from God with your personal address on it," as Sören Kierkegaard once put it. We shall read it as a story which is not just about other people of long ago but which is about us in the places where we are living. The language of the Bible, when it is truly heard, can be an event, a happening, such as it was with biblical witnesses, like Moses, who first were addressed personally by the God of Abraham, Isaac, and Jacob.

■ God's Manifesto

The uniqueness of this Bible Study, which emphasizes the reader's identification with the plot of the story, arises from the uniqueness of the Bible itself. It is the Christian claim that the perspective set forth in the Bible has been provided by God through his own self-revelation. This is what puts the Bible in a class by itself. The Bible is not written in a secret code, but in living human language which reveals the dramatic involvement of God in our personal lives and in our history. Christians affirm that the Bible contains the Word of God. Just as in our everyday experience a "word" is an event of communication between persons, so likewise God's Word is an event of communication, the act of his taking part in the reality of our history, as we read in John 1:14 ("The Word became flesh and dwelt among us . . ."). This dynamic power of God's Word is a far cry from the notion that the Bible contains the literal, static words of God taken down by human stenographers. The Bible is not divine dictation, but divine drama whose language poetically exposes the meaning of human life in relation to the God who has condescended to dwell among us, in our human language and history. The Bible is, to cite the title of a fairly recent book, "Word of God in words of men." [1]

The Bible may be described as "God's Manifesto." The dictionary defines a manifesto as "a public declaration, usually of a sovereign or political group, showing intentions and motives." So, for instance, the Communist Manifesto is a declaration of the alleged meaning of man's economic history and the predetermined movement of the historical process toward fulfillment in a classless society. To be a Communist is to understand one's existence in this context. In a more special sense the Bible is, for the Christian community, God's

[1] This point is amplified in my *Rediscovering the Bible* (Association Press, 1951), chap. 1. See also the book (written from a Roman Catholic perspective) by Jean Levie, *The Bible: Word of God in Words of Men* (Kenedy, 1962) and that of Claus Westermann, *Our Controversial Bible* (Augsburg Publishing House, 1969), chapter 12.

Manifesto. God is the Sovereign who declares the inner meaning of a historical crisis and discloses the direction of the whole human drama. His revelation is given in the events of which the Bible is the record and the witness, events which come to climax and fulfillment in Jesus Christ. And to be a Christian is to understand one's existence in this dramatic context.

Now, this does not mean that one has to be a convinced Christian before he can get anything out of the study of the Bible. As Paul Lehmann once observed, "The Bible has a curious slant in favor of the unbeliever; the unbeliever, that is, who is really honest about his unbelief, and really curious about the full diversity and complexity of the world in which he lives." [2] The only condition for fruitful Bible Study is that you come with an infinite concern about the question: "What is the meaning of my life, and the historical crisis in which I and my community are involved?" Instead of saying with Henry Ford that "history is bunk," you must be willing to let the past—this biblical past—speak to you where you are living, to make a claim upon you in the present. You must meet others in the group as persons, respecting their individuality and being willing to learn from the conversation. You must come with the intention of wrestling seriously and honestly with the meaning of a biblical passage—not to air your private

[2] Paul Lehmann, *The Death of Jesus Christ: A Bible Study on What Led Christians to Study the Bible* (United Student Christian Council, 1951).

opinions or prejudices. You must be ready to hear what the great teachers of the Church have had to say in their commentaries—Augustine, Calvin, Luther, and others, including those of our own period. In short, you must expect to be questioned by the Bible, even as you bring your own questions to the Bible. It may be that in this give-and-take experience you will discover an entirely new dimension of life, as you find yourself drawn into the history which God is making.

■ The Bible as a Whole

In the following studies we shall tackle the whole Bible. This may seem as foolish as American tourists who breeze through the Louvre Museum in Paris as though they are trying to establish a new track record. It is admitted at the outset that this approach runs the risk of superficiality. Let's hope that you will have time enough to stake your claims so that later you can come back to sink your shafts more deeply, aided perhaps by the "Suggestions for Further Reading" given at the end of each study unit. Most of us, however, lack any awareness of the Bible as a whole. We know a few snatches of Scripture here and there, like the Twenty-third Psalm or the Sermon on the Mount, but are very hazy—if not completely ignorant— about the larger dramatic context within which these favorite passages have meaning. We need to stand back from the trees so that we may see the

erent historical situations, different kinds of theological expression. But underlying all this great
variety is the dynamic movement, similar to the
plot of a drama, which binds the whole together.
The biblical drama, however, is unique in that God
appears in the cast. Not only is he the Author who
stands behind the scenes prompting and directing
the drama, but he enters onto the stage of history
as the Chief Actor—the protagonist. The biblical
plot is the working out of God's purpose for his
creation in spite of all efforts to oppose it. The
denouement is reached, according to the conviction of the Christian community, when the Crucifixion and Resurrection of Jesus of Nazareth is
proclaimed as the sign of God's decisive victory.
In the light of this climactic event the earlier stages
of the story are understood with a deeper and
larger meaning.

■ A Drama in Three Acts

Using this dramatic scheme, the eight studies in
this series may be outlined as follows:

Prologue: In the Beginning (STUDY I)

Act I: The Formation of God's People
   Scene 1: A Way into the Future (STUDY II)
   Scene 2: The Discipline of Disaster
       (STUDY III)

Act II: The Re-formation of God's People
   Scene 1: The New Exodus (STUDY IV)
   Scene 2: The People of the Torah (STUDY V)

Act III: The Transformation of God's People
   Scene 1: Victory Through Defeat
         (STUDY VI)
   Scene 2: The Church in the World
         (STUDY VII)

Epilogue: In the End (STUDY VIII)

In the course of these studies it will become clear that each of the major *Acts* interprets a decisive historical event which is proclaimed as a "mighty act" of God. The three crucial moments in the biblical drama are:

1. The exodus of oppressed Israelites from Egypt and the opening of a way into the future out of a no-exit situation.
2. The exile of conquered Israelites into Babylonia and their miraculous liberation for a new beginning in their homeland.
3. The crucifixion and resurrection of Jesus which reconstituted the People of God as his task force in the world.

The selection of passages for the study of these three major "acts" of God has to be somewhat arbitrary, for obviously we can deal with only a small fraction of the relevant biblical material.[4] Our purpose is not to make an exhaustive study of the Bible, but to enter into the meaning of these three crucial stages of the biblical drama.

[4] Four passages are selected for each study unit. If cnly one session is devoted to each unit, the leader will have to determine which passage should be the focus of discussion. Otherwise, the group may want to stay with a particular unit for more than one session.

■ Getting Into the Act

One final word: don't suppose that this is the kind of drama we can view from a grandstand seat. We are not to be spectators of something that happened once upon a time. The Bible is not a book of ancient history. It is more like the commedia dell'arte, a dramatic form which flourished in sixteenth century Italy. In this kind of drama, the players were asked to improvise, to put themselves into the story. To be sure, it was not a free improvisation, for there were some given elements: there was the director, there was a company of actors, and there was a story plot which was given to them in broad outline. With these given elements they were told to improvise—that is, to fill in the gaps on their own.

In this Bible Study *we* are called upon to improvise—that is, to put ourselves into the story and to fill in the gaps with our own experience. We must be ready to get onto the biblical stage and participate personally—along with the "company," the community of faith—in the dramatic movement of the plot, act by act. Perhaps this warning is unnecessary, for it is the testimony of experience that as one reads the Bible the Holy Spirit convinces the reader that God speaks to him

---

[5] See my essay on "The Contemporaneity of the Bible," *Princeton Seminary Bulletin*, Vol. LXII (1969), pp. 38–50, where this point is developed, with reference to the commedia dell'arte.

personally and makes him an actor in the drama. Paul Minear has put the matter this way:

> It is as if in the theater, where I am hugely enjoying an esthetic view of life, God interrupts the show with a stentorian announcement: "Is John Smith in the house?" And I am John Smith. And the interruption continues: "Report immediately . . . for a task intended for you alone." [6]

So, realizing that God, the Director, is apt to stop the show at any moment and put us into the act, let's begin our study.

Suggestions for Further Study

Herberg, Will, "Biblical Faith as *Heilsgeschichte:* The Meaning of Redemptive History in Human Existence," *The Christian Scholar,* Vol. 39 (1956), pp. 25–31. An important, penetrating treatment of the narrative character of biblical faith.

Niebuhr, H. Richard, *The Meaning of Revelation* (Macmillan, 1941), especially chapter 2 ("The Story of Our Life") which emphasizes the narrative mode of the Christian confession of faith.

Wright, G. Ernest, *God Who Acts: Biblical Theology as Recital* (SCM Press, 1952; 7th impression 1964). A widely influential exposition of biblical theology as the recital of the acts of God.

[6] Paul S. Minear, *Eyes of Faith,* rev. ed. (Westminster, 1966), pp. 42–43.

THE UNFOLDING DRAMA
OF THE BIBLE

STUDY I

PROLOGUE:
IN THE BEGINNING

STUDY PASSAGES:

1. Genesis 1:1 through 2:4a (first half of verse)
   The Creation of the World

2. Psalm 8
   Man in God's Creation

3. Psalm 104
   The Wonderful Order of Creation

4. Genesis 2:4b (second half of verse) through 3:24
   Paradise Lost

One of the daringly original themes of the biblical drama is expressed in the majestic announcement of the first words of Genesis: "In the beginning God created the heavens and the earth." We are so used to speaking of God as Creator that we scarcely realize the revolutionary implications of this belief. According to the religions of ancient Egypt and Babylonia the gods were in nature, for nature with its creative powers was regarded as a manifestation of the divine. In Babylonia, for instance, Creation was seen to be part of a natural process which moves in a great circle toward the New Creation at the turn of the year, the time of the New Year's festival. Likewise for the ancient Greeks the gods were immanent or "inside" nature, and since the world was regarded as being eternal there was no place in their thought for Creation. The Bible stands in flat contradiction to these views. God is not in nature; He is not a natural process. Rather, God is "over against" nature, and nature displays the handiwork of her Creator (Psalm 19:1). Heaven and earth (this is, all that is) are seen to be part of the majestic purpose of God which moves in a vast sweep from beginning to end, from Creation to Consummation.[1]

---

[1] For further elucidation of Israel's creation-belief in relation to that of ancient religions see my *Creation versus Chaos* (Association Press, 1967), especially chapter 1, "Creation and History."

■ Life's Deepest Dimension

A roadblock which stands in the way of our approach to Genesis 1–3 is our slavery to the scientific attitude. Too many people try to modernize these chapters into a scientific account, and to harmonize the narrative with modern scientific theories. Some have argued, for instance, that the "days" mentioned in Genesis 1 correspond to geological periods, or that the doctrine of evolution is implicit in the whole account. But this is to miss the whole point of the biblical language. The central issue here is that of the *historical meaning* of man's life in the natural world, and this is not a scientific question, properly speaking. The Bible asks—and answers—the *ultimate* question: "what is the origin, meaning, and destiny of man's life?" You must be on guard against reading into the biblical narrative the presuppositions of our scientific age. It would be advisable to read the creation account in Genesis 1 in the context of some of the Psalms, especially Psalms 8 and 104. This is poetic language which intends to praise the God whose purpose enfolds all things and upon whom every creature is radically dependent for existence (see Psalm 104:27–30).[2]

It is now generally known that actually we have two narratives of the Creation, the first running from Genesis 1:1 to the first part of Genesis 2:4,

[2] See the chapter on "Creation and Worship," in *Creation versus Chaos*.

and the second beginning with the last half of Genesis 2:4. The first of these accounts received its final literary formulation in the period we are symbolizing as *Act II* (about 550 B.C.), although it was probably used liturgically in the Temple services long before its final composition. The second account, on the other hand, comes from the period of *Act I,* perhaps as early as the era of Solomon (about 950 B.C.). Both stories reflect the meaning of these *Acts* of the biblical drama, just as they reflect the language and culture of their period.[3] The important thing to notice, however, is that despite their differences in style and content, both accounts affirm that the meaning of human life is not disclosed in nature but in relationship to the God who transcends the natural world. God is the Author, Sustainer, and Finisher of all that is. These stories are really word pictures which portray life's deepest dimension.[4]

It would be helpful if we had in the English language two words which correspond to German *Weltbild* ("world picture") and *Weltanschauung* ("world perspective"). The world picture of Genesis 1 is the naive one of antiquity: a picture of the earth as a flat surface, resting on the pri-

[3] For a fuller discussion of the place of these two accounts in the history of Israelite tradition, see *Rediscovering the Bible,* pp. 43–52; also my *Understanding the Old Testament,* 2nd ed. (Prentice-Hall, 1966), pp. 160–187 and pp. 378–393.

[4] Alan Richardson has a good discussion of the pictorial meaning of these stories, in *Genesis I–XI,* Torch Commentary (SCM Press, 1953).

meval "waters beneath the earth" and separated
from "the waters above the earth" by a blue
firmament (Genesis 2:6–7). Were it not for the
Creator's sustaining power, the waters would return to their original place and engulf the world
in chaos, as almost happened during the Flood
(Genesis 6:5–9:17). The world perspective, however, concerns the meaning of man's life on the
natural stage and in relation to his ecological
environment, organic and inorganic. Man is able
to survey and control nature, to search for the
good, the true, and the beautiful, to remember the
past, to hope for the future, and to decide in
the present. Elevated to a royal position "a little
lower than God" (Psalm 8:5–8), man is God's
highest creature on earth. Significantly he is "made
in the image of God," which means that he is
God's *representative* on earth, singled out to rule
wisely and benevolently over the creatures of his
earthly environment. Notice that man and animals
are created on the same day (Genesis 1:24–28) —
a fine poetic indication of man's dependence upon
his natural environment.[5]

The story in Genesis 2 is written from a similar
perspective. Like the animals, man is made from
the dust and returns to the dust; but his ability to
name the animals indicates his dominion over the
animal kingdom (2:19–20). Today we know
about the chemical constituents of this dust, and

[5] See the perceptive essay by Karlfried Froehlich on
"The Ecology of Creation," *Theology Today,* Vol. XXVII,
No. 3 (1970), pp. 263–276.

we have a much more complete world picture corresponding to our space age. But have we gone beyond the biblical perspective on the meaning of man's life in relationship to his natural environment? [6]

Herbert Butterfield, once a professor of modern history at the university of Cambridge, has written some words which are relevant to the Creation story:

> The historian does not treat man as the student of biology seems to—does not regard him as essentially a part of nature or consider him primarily in this aspect. He picks up the other end of the stick and envisages a world of human relations standing, so to speak, over against nature—he studies that new kind of life which man has superimposed on the jungle, the forest and the waste. Since this world of human relations is the historian's universe, we may say that history is a human drama of personalities, taking place, as it were, on the stage of nature, and amid its imposing scenery.[7]

Thus we speak of the human drama, although often in purely humanistic terms. The Creation story underscores the conviction that the drama is not just about man, for it has its beginning and end in the purpose of God. History is *His*–Story.

[6] See the discussion of myths of the beginning, in *Rediscovering the Bible,* pp. 236–248. Alan Richardson, in *The Bible in the Age of Science* (Westminster Press, 1961) indicates that the so-called conflict between science and religion results from a failure to understand the true character of the biblical message.

[7] Herbert Butterfield, *Christianity and History* (Charles Scribner's Sons, 1950), pp. 6–7. Used by permission.

■ Paradise Lost

You should devote much of your attention to the narrative of Paradise Lost in Genesis 2 and 3, for in this story are to be found the profoundest insights into the human problem. Don't be disturbed by the picturesque and naive style of the language, as though this marked the story as inferior to that of Genesis 1. These chapters focus upon God's personal relation to man, and we have no other language to portray this relationship except the rich symbols of human speech. You should reflect on the meaning of some of these symbols: the Tree of Life, Adam's rib, the serpent, the forbidden fruit, nakedness, and so forth. Read the story with poetic imagination.

This is not just a story of something that happened once upon a time, but is a profound description of the human situation in any historical time. Indeed, the word *'Adam* in Hebrew is really not a proper name but is a generic term for "man, mankind." Adam represents Everyman. Surely there is in human experience a melancholy awareness that man's life is not what it ought to be, that somehow or somewhere he has lost the peace, the wholeness, the humanity which the Creator intended. Conflict, anxiety, insecurity, exploitation, injustice, suffering—these are not intended to be normal, even though they are life's daily realities. Why is this? Unlike Marxism, which traces the problem to economic factors, and unlike Oriental religions (Hinduism, Buddhism), which see man

caught in a realm of sensory illusion, the Bible
traces the problem to man's estrangement from the
purpose of God, to man's will.[8]

Notice that the Adam story falls into three
episodes:

A. In the first episode Adam is the *gardener*.
He has a God-given task: to dress and keep the
garden in faithfulness to his Creator. Work, when
performed in trust and responsibility, is man's
God-given dignity. Man is not created to violate
and pollute nature but to be the caretaker of God's
garden.

B. In the second episode Adam is the *rebel*. His
freedom makes it possible for him to obey or to
disobey God's sovereign will, and he cannot resist
the tempting possibilities of life on his own terms.
The meaning of the phrase "knowing good and
evil" is not altogether clear, but it seems to be a
Hebrew expression for the mature and even divine
wisdom required for making difficult decisions
(see I Kings 3:9; II Samuel 14:17). Sin, then, is
man's presumption that he can grasp such wide
and penetrating knowledge that he can live on his
own resources, without dependence upon God.
Sin is man's declaration of independence from
God, man's refusal to "let God be God." Above
all, we must understand that sin is not just a matter
of doing something immoral, of being bad boys
and girls. Sin is man's false maturity. It is alienation from God, from one's fellow men, and from

[8] See further in *Rediscovering the Bible*, pp. 248–254;
Creation versus Chaos, chapter 5, especially pp. 155–159.

one's truest self—an alienation which is rooted in a rebellious will that oversteps creaturely limitations.[9]

C. In the third episode Adam is the *fugitive*—hiding in vain behind the trees of the garden and finally cast out from the primeval peace of paradise into a restless historical life of insecurity and conflict. The rest of the Bible, beginning with the tragic story portrayed in Genesis 4–11, is a commentary on the truth that when men are estranged from God they are separated from their fellow men and from their deepest selves. For man belongs to God by nature, and cannot find peace outside the relationship of dependence for which he was created. So Augustine began his *Confessions* with this prayer: "O Lord, thou hast made us for thyself, and our hearts are restless until they rest in thee."

QUESTIONS TO THINK ABOUT

1. Discuss the difference between the "truth" of the biblical account of creation and the "truth" which we usually regard as scientific. Was it appropriate for astronauts to broadcast as their Christmas message from the moon (Christmas 1968) the opening verses of Genesis?

2. At a recent conference on ecology (the relation of man to his environment) a speaker maintained

[9] See Paul Tillich's sermon, "You are Accepted," in *The Shaking of the Foundations* (Charles Scribner's Sons, 1948), chapter 19.

that Christianity is largely responsible for the present "rape of nature," because in Genesis 1:26–28 man is empowered to have dominion over nature. Discuss this thesis in the light of man as the "image" (representative) of God (Genesis 1) or man as the "gardener" (Genesis 2).

3. With the story of Genesis 2–3 before you, paraphrase the meaning of "sin." Can sin find expression in moral goodness as well as in immoral acts? What light, if any, does Albert Camus' novel, *The Fall,* throw on the story?

4. A British observer, James Bryce, once observed that the American Constitution, with its system of checks and balances upon the exercise of power, was written by men who believed in "original sin." Is this realistic? Compare the Marxist view that the troubles of history are traceable to economic factors, and that when these are changed human nature will be transformed. (George Orwell's *Animal Farm* may give some food for thought.)

5. Compare the picture of creation presented in Genesis 1 with that of Psalm 104. Why is the story in Genesis 2–3 (Paradise Lost) a necessary supplement to the view of man in God's creation as set forth in Genesis 1?

Suggestions for Further Reading

Anderson, Bernhard W., *The Beginning of History,* Bible Guides (Lutterworth, Abingdon, 1963); *Creation versus Chaos* (Association Press, 1967), especially chapters 1–3.

Fritsch, Charles T., *Genesis,* Layman's Bible Commentaries (John Knox Press, 1959). A brief, helpful introduction.

von Rad, Gerhard, *Genesis,* Old Testament Library (Westminster, 1961). An excellent commentary; highly recommended.

Sarna, Nahum, *Understanding Genesis* (McGraw-Hill, 1966). A clear and illuminating exposition by a Jewish scholar.

A WAY INTO THE FUTURE

STUDY PASSAGES:

1. Exodus 3:1–21
   The Call of Moses

2. Exodus 19:3–6 and 20:1–17
   Keeping the Covenant

3. Exodus 24:3–8
   Ceremony of Covenant-making

4. Deuteronomy 4:25–40; 5:1–53;
   8:1–20
   Sermonic Interpretations of
   Exodus and Covenant

With the Exodus, or the "going out," of the Israelites from Egypt, the curtain rises on the first major Act of the biblical drama. Every historical community recalls some decisive event as its birth hour. Of this formative event the members of the community can say: "This is what brought us forth upon the stage of history as a people, with a shared tradition and destiny. This is where the meaning of our history was disclosed." In the United States, for instance, Americans celebrate the Revolutionary War and the Declaration of Independence as decisive events in the formation of that people. It is significant that in a grave crisis Abraham Lincoln harked back to that creative moment: "Fourscore and seven years ago our fathers brought forth on this continent a new nation, conceived in liberty . . ."

■ Israel's Birth-Hour

It was similar in the case of the community known as Israel, to which the Church is intimately related.[1] However, the analogy of America and Israel breaks down at this point. For Israel the Exodus was not just a creative event, but the event of God's calling a people into relationship with him.

[1] The term "Israel" was used of the People of God before a state was formed under David (ca. 1000 B.C.). Therefore we must be on guard against an easy identification of the Israel of the Old Testament with the modern secular state of Israel. The existence of this modern state lies beyond the pale of our present discussion.

> When Israel was a child, I loved him,
> and out of Egypt I called my son.
>   —Hosea 11:1

The Exodus was a time of encounter with the Lord of history. Israel's ancient confession of faith found expression in the retelling of a story in which the Exodus was the focal event. The confession ran something like this: "Our forefathers were pilgrims in Palestine, wandering from place to place. A small band went down to Egypt in a time of famine, and when Israel multiplied, the Egyptian king subjected *us* to slave labor on public works. But the Lord, the God of our fathers, saw *our* affliction and heard *our* cry. With many marvellous signs of his presence in our midst, he delivered *us* from Pharaoh's yoke, and brought us into a new land where we could find our freedom in serving him." In this paraphrase of Deuteronomy 26:5–9, note how the individual worshipper identifies himself with the story, as evidenced in the first personal pronouns *our, us*. Even today the Passover ceremony emphasizes the involvement of the believing Jew in that momentous event.

These crucial events, especially the central event of the Exodus, exerted a powerful influence upon the religious imagination of the people in the new situations in which they found themselves in their historical pilgrimage. The God whom Israel worships is the God who comes to his people in the time of oppression and opens a way into the future where there is no way. The imagery of the Israelite story has had a great appeal to Christians in many ages, as witnessed most recently by the preaching of Martin Luther King, whose "dream" for America was infused with the imagery of liberation from Pharaoh's yoke and a march through the wilderness toward the promised land.[2]

The best way to prepare for this study is to read as much as possible of Exodus 1–24 and the later commentary on the meaning of these events found in Deuteronomy 1–11. Here our primary concern is not with critical details.[3] Rather, we want to enter into the inner meaning of the Exodus drama —the meaning which was kept alive and relived in every annual celebration of the Passover Feast and in periodic covenant-renewal services at the central sanctuary (Joshua 24). This can be done by concentrating on the passages that have been selected, perhaps with side reference to the sermonic material in Deuteronomy 4:25–40 or 8:1–20. It would be advisable to bypass the question of particular miracle stories for the time being (*e.g.,* the plagues) and concentrate on the central miracle of "the mystery of Israel"—the elected people that has survived to this day.

[2] An excellent discussion of Martin Luther King's use of biblical imagery is given by James H. Smylie in "On Jesus, Pharaohs, and the Chosen People: Martin Luther King as Biblical Interpreter and Humanist," *Interpretation* XXIV (1970), pp. 74–91.

[3] For a discussion of literary and historical problems, see my *Understanding the Old Testament,* 2nd edition (Prentice-Hall, 1966), chapters 1 and 2. See also the elaboration of the meaning of the Exodus in *Rediscovering the Bible,* chapter 3.

■ God Introduces Himself

A good place to begin the discussion is the story of
Moses' call in Exodus 3, for this narrative presents the theme of the whole Book of Exodus.
Rather than tripping over literal details, read the
passage with religious imagination. Perhaps you
will find that the dialogue sounds deep notes in
your own experience. Notice that Moses was
brought into an "I–Thou" relation to God not as
he was overwhelmed by the grandeur of nature
but as he was brooding over the meaning of a
historical situation: the plight of his kinsmen who
were crying out under oppression in Egypt. Ob-
serve the emphasis upon God's entrance into the
historical struggle: "I have seen the plight of my
people" . . . "I have heard their cry" . . . "I know
their sorrows" . . . "I have come down to rescue
them." The God of the Exodus is not removed
from where men are struggling and suffering; he
is here, actively opening a way into the future.

The story of Moses' encounter with God is
paralleled in other accounts, as in the story of
Elijah at Mt. Horeb (Sinai) (I Kings 19), the call
of a prophet (see Isaiah 6; Amos 7:10–17), the
psalmist's awareness of the inescapable God
(Psalm 139), or the symphony of voices in the
New Testament which affirm that God has spoken
to men through Jesus Christ. Therefore, when we
speak of "revelation" we are referring to a personal encounter in which God reveals *himself* and
thereby exposes the meaning of human existence.

God introduces himself, so to speak; he makes himself known through his word and his action. Perhaps a human analogy will help to clarify this. We cannot really know any person unless he reveals himself to us through his speech and actions. We can know a lot of things *about* John Jones: his family background, his education, his job, his physical appearance, and so on; but we cannot really know John Jones himself unless he chooses to disclose his inner self through what he says and does. So it is with God. We cannot know God himself unless he chooses to reveal himself in prophetic word and historical action. "Revelation" is not receiving ideas about God, but is rather to meet God, to be introduced to God personally. And the meeting place is the concrete life situations of our history.[4]

■ God's Personal Name

One interesting motif of the Moses story is the giving of God's name. In the ancient world a personal name was not just a label, as it usually is for us, but was closely connected with the person of the bearer. A person's name was believed to be a disclosure of his identity and nature. Moses, we are told, was reluctant to go back to

[4] Some classic discussions of this subject are: Martin Buber, *I and Thou* (T. & T. Clark, 1937); also his *Eclipse of God* (Harper and Brothers, 1952); further, H. Richard Niebuhr, *The Meaning of Revelation* (Macmillan, 1941).

Egypt, lest his kinsman ask the name of the God who had commissioned him. In this context we read about the disclosure—though with some reticence—of God's name, for "I am who I am" is a word play upon the Israelite personal name of God (Yahweh).[5] The narrative wants to stress that God gives *himself* (his name) to his people; he is truly present with them. But his name cannot be used for human purposes, as in some primitive religions the knowledge of a person's name is used to gain magical control over him. The God of Israel, who makes himself known in the event of the Exodus, is not subject to the control and manipulation of his people. He condescends to be with his people and to go with them, but he is not "their God" in a possessive sense—the prisoner of their thoughts or national ambitions. The God of Israel keeps the initiative as he leads his people into the future; and invariably he introduces surprises which demand a reconsideration of what men had believed in the past. The great prophets (*e.g.,* Amos, Hosea, Isaiah, Jeremiah) announced these divine surprises in their time with shocking impact. And perhaps the greatest surprise of all came with the New Testament announcement that God was present in Jesus of Nazareth, in his life, death, and resurrection.

[5] In the Revised Standard Version the sacred name is translated "the Lord," following synagogue practice. For a clear and profound discussion of the giving of God's name see Gerhard von Rad, *Moses,* World Christian Books (Lutterworth, Association Press, 1960), pp. 18–25.

Christ's mission, according to the Gospel of John, was to manifest God's name (John 17:6).

■ The Covenant Commitment

The next three passages (Exodus 19:3–6, 20:1–17, and 24:3–8) should be considered together, for they deal with Israel's response to God's intervention on her behalf. Here we come upon the central motif of the biblical drama: the Covenant (Old Testament really means "Old Covenant"; New Testament, "New Covenant"). As in the case of the marriage covenant this biblical covenant is a personal relationship based on commitment and trust. Unlike the marriage covenant, however, it is more unilateral in character, for it is a covenant between unequals—God and man. It is God who "makes" or "gives" the Covenant, and Israel who responds in gratitude, reverence, and loyalty.

Much light has been shed upon the nature of the Mosaic covenant from ancient treaties or covenants which governed the relations between peoples during the period before David. Among the archives of the ancient Hittites (a people who ruled in Asia Minor, which is modern Turkey, from 1600 to 1200 B.C.) archaeologists have found copies of treaties between the Hittite suzerain and vassal states. The treaty form includes several major elements. To begin with, the Great King announces his name and titles and declares the benevolent deeds he has performed on behalf of the vassal state. There follows a list of stipulations which are binding upon the vassal in gratitude for favors received, including the prohibition of entering into foreign alliances. Then, for the vassal who takes the oath of loyalty, these legal stipulations are sanctioned by the invocation of blessing and curse—blessing for obedience and curse (judgment) for betrayal of the covenant. The treaty form also included a provision for periodic public reading of the covenant laws and the renewal of the vows of allegiance.[6]

In many respects the covenant between God and Israel is similar to this ancient covenant form, showing that Israel used a prevalent literary vehicle to confess her faith in the God who claimed his people in the event of the Exodus. Israel, however, put a new picture into the old frame. The following points deserve your consideration:

1. God takes the initiative in establishing this covenant relationship. He intervenes into the historical situation with the disclosure of his name (Who God is) and his acts of benevolence toward his people. Israel did not choose, but was *chosen*. Therefore, faith is wholehearted response to God's initiative as manifested in his "mighty act" of deliverance which opened a way into the future.

2. This relationship places men under a cate-

---

[6] An admirable, nontechnical discussion of the Mosaic covenant in the light of ancient political treaties is found in Delbert Hillers, *Covenant: The History of a Biblical Idea* (Johns Hopkins Press, 1969).

gorical demand: "Thou shalt" or "Thou shalt not." In the Decalog God addresses his people in absolute terms, and they are responsible to him in all the relationships of life. One cannot serve God with half his heart, and some other loyalty with the other half of his devotion. Like any absolute commitment, the covenant allegiance is essentially a jealous one.

3. The covenant involves not only obligations toward God, but obligations toward the other members of the community. This is the meaning of the giving of the Law (Torah) in connection with the making of the covenant. The legal stipulations were adapted to new cultural circumstances, but the basic principle remained constant: Men are absolutely responsible to one another because they are absolutely responsible to God.

4. Ethical responsibility is motivated by gratitude for *what God has done*—that is, his self-revelation and his acts of benevolence manifested in the event of the Exodus. Notice the preface to the Ten Commandments: "I am the Lord [Yahweh] your God, who brought you out of the land of Egypt, out of the house of bondage." Men are to obey God not as slaves driven to their duties, but as people who stand in awe and gratitude before the gracious deeds of their Redeemer.

5. The Mosaic covenant contains a conditional element: *"If* you will obey my voice and keep my covenant . . ." (Exodus 19:3–6). Faithfulness to the covenant yields blessing, betrayal brings the curse of divine judgment. This element of the

covenant was picked up later by the great prophets of Israel.

■ Chosen for Service

It is important to see how the Exodus story ties in with the dramatic sequence of the Book of Genesis. As we saw in the last study, Genesis 1–3 gives a word picture of the fundamental human situation: man's estrangement from God in spite of his supreme position as God's representative on earth. The consequences of the human tragedy are spelled out in the stories of Genesis 4–11, in which things go from bad to worse. Then we are told in Genesis 12:1–3 that God, to meet this universal human predicament, took appropriate action by calling a man (Abraham) and promising him that his people would be the means of blessing to all the broken and divided families of mankind. The God who speaks to Moses is "the God of the fathers"— *i.e.,* Abraham, Isaac, and Jacob. Thus the deliverance of the Israelites from Egyptian bondage is seen in the perspective of God's redemptive concern to bring mankind to the full measure of humanity intended in the Creation.

QUESTIONS TO THINK ABOUT

1. Some religions (*e.g.,* Hinduism) maintain that Ultimate Reality is Unnamable; attempts to name God reduce the divine to the level of human distinctions or domesticate the divine in the realm of change

and decay. Against this view, how would you understand the story of God's giving his Name to his people?

2. Does it make sense in our time to say that "God acts in history"? Do you think that Exodus 3:7–8 describes God's involvement with suppressed and exploited peoples today?

3. A justice of the Supreme Court defended a decision by saying that in modern society "there are no absolutes." How does a "situational ethic" square with the covenant faith? Would you say that the Ten Commandments are absolutely binding in every situation?

4. "Thou shalt have no other gods before me." What does God's "jealousy" mean in our situation? What are some of the "gods" that men worship today?

5. A fundamental premise of the Bible, both Old and New Testaments, is that God has "chosen" a people to serve him. According to your present understanding, discuss the meaning of the election of Israel (or the Church).

Suggestions for Further Reading

Mendenhall, George, *Law and Covenant in Israel and the Ancient Near East* (Pittsburgh: Biblical Colloquium, 1955). A pioneering study in Israel's covenant tradition in the light of Hittite parallels. See also his later article on "Covenant" in the *Interpreter's Dictionary of the Bible*.

Napier, B. D., *Exodus,* Layman's Bible Commentary (John Knox Press, 1963). A clear introduction which communicates like a good sermon.

Newman, Murray L. Jr., *The People of the Covenant* (Abingdon, 1962). An illuminating study of two covenant theologies which arose in the period before David.

Plastaras, James, *The God of Exodus: The Theology of the Exodus Narratives* (Bruce, 1966). A valuable discussion of the centrality of the Exodus in the Bible by a Roman Catholic scholar.

Wright, G. Ernest, "Introduction to and Exegesis of the Book of Deuteronomy," in *The Interpreter's Bible,* Vol. II (Abingdon, 1953). One of the best treatments of the Book of Deuteronomy.

This is a study in tragedy. During Jeremiah's long career as a prophet in Jerusalem (626–587 B.C.), events move swiftly and inexorably toward the precipice of disaster. The very foundations shake under the shattering impact of ominous historical events. And finally the curtain of the first main Act of the biblical drama comes down on a scene of utter ruin: the Temple is destroyed, the nation has fallen, and the cream of the population has been carried away into foreign exile. "By the waters of Babylon, there we sat down and wept, when we remembered Zion [Jerusalem]," lamented a psalmist (Psalm 137:1).

■ The People that Walked in Darkness

To appreciate the full pathos of the tragedy let's telescope Israel's history from the Exodus to the fall of the nation into a short summary. After the miraculous deliverance from Egypt the Israelites were forged into a community in the experiences of the desert where, despite their murmurings, they repeatedly experienced the grace and the faithfulness of God (Exodus 16–18; Numbers 10–36). With a sense of God-given destiny, kept alive through the memory of the saving event of the Exodus and the covenant of Sinai, they moved into the Promised Land. There, under the leadership of Joshua and his successors, they successfully maintained a foothold despite enemy pressure. For some generations the people were bound together in a tribal confederacy known as "Israel."

During this period (the two centuries before David) the people came together periodically on occasions of worship to renew their covenantal allegiance to the God who had shown his benevolent power in the Exodus. As on the occasion of the great convocation at Shechem under Joshua (Joshua 24), they heard anew the marvelous story of what God had done, they listened to the public reading of the stipulations of the covenant, and they renewed their covenant vow to serve the God of the Exodus and to be obedient to his word. The formula of Exodus 24:7 was echoed in these services of covenant renewal: "All that the Lord has spoken we will do, and we will be obedient."

In time the community Israel became a nation, and under the leadership of David rose to a height of prestige and glory. This new development was regarded in some circles as the continuation and outcome of what God had started to do in the period of the Exodus. Royal theologians advanced the view that God had entered into a special covenant with Israel *through David* the king, a covenant which guaranteed social stability and the continuity of the Davidic dynasty (II Samuel 7). The story of God's saving actions, begun in the Exodus, was seen to point toward the special choice of David and of Zion in the divine purpose (see Psalm 78, especially verses 67–72). In other words, God was continuing to lead his people into the future.

Troubles soon broke out, however. Under the oppressive reign of David's son, Solomon, there was great restiveness beneath the surface of the nation's glory, and at his death the volcano of revolution erupted. The once united kingdom was split into North and South by civil strife, the former clinging to the Mosaic tradition and the latter emphasizing the covenant with David. The people of Israel, torn apart by fratricidal rivalry and warfare, were soon caught in the power struggle of the ancient Near East. Crushed beneath the heel of the conqueror, the Northern Kingdom was destroyed by the Assyrians in 722 B.C., and the Southern Kingdom was finished off by the Babylonians in the fateful year 587 B.C.

■ The Contemporaneity of the Covenant

During this tumultuous period there appeared a remarkable succession of prophets—men like Samuel, Elijah, Amos, Hosea, Isaiah, Jeremiah, and Ezekiel. In all ancient history there was nothing that matched the succession of prophets who arose in Israel. Today many people suppose that a prophet is a clairvoyant who peers into a crystal ball, as it were, and discloses the shape of things to come. This, however, is a caricature of prophecy. The true prophet was one who interpreted the meaning of the historical crisis in the light of Israel's covenant loyalty. The prophets were not extremists who introduced radically new conceptions which broke with the past; nor were they reactionaries who merely repeated the old traditions in a new time. Rather, they spoke to the

urgent and imperative present of the community
by reinterpreting the meaning of the covenant
traditions in the present crisis and by warning the
people of the consequences of their action for the
future.[1]

The tense that matters most in Israel's faith is
the present, the *today* of the covenant. This con-
temporaneous note, frequently heard on occasions
of worship in the Israelite community, is sounded
in a passage in Deuteronomy which serves as an
introduction to the Decalog:

> The Lord our God made a covenant with us in
> Horeb [Sinai].
> Not with our fathers did the Lord make this cove-
> nant, but with us, who are all of us here alive
> this day.
>
> —Deuteronomy 5:2–3

If the prophets speak to us today, it is because in
our time the present is qualitatively the same, even
though the date is in the twentieth century.

■ The Trial of Israel

For this study we have arbitrarily selected Jeremiah as representative of the prophetic movement,

[1] Here it would be helpful to turn to the discussion of
the prophet Hosea by Walter Brueggemann, *Tradition
for Crisis* (John Knox, 1968), where it is pointed out
that the prophets reinterpreted the old traditions to make
them relevant for the present. Incidentally, there are
many close affinities between the northern prophet Hosea
and Jeremiah who prophesied in the south about a century later.

and a few passages from the Book of Jeremiah as representative of the prophet's message.[2] During his career (about 626–587 B.C.) Jeremiah saw the colossal Assyrian empire disintegrate; he witnessed the intense nationalism of the Southern Kingdom, fanned by the patriotic hope for independence; he beheld the new Babylonian empire rise from the ashes of Assyria and spread destruction throughout Palestine. What was the meaning of these events? Like prophets who preceded him (for instance, Hosea in the middle of the eighth century B.C.), Jeremiah insisted that disaster was a form of discipline—that is, God was "teaching" his people through these tragic events (as the word *discipline* literally suggests). God was actively confronting his people on the plane of history, leading them through suffering to a new beginning in his grace. Therefore, even though there was tragedy, it was *meaningful* tragedy.

The selected passages form a good sequence for discussion. The first one (Jeremiah 1:4–19) describes Jeremiah's commission in a dialogue which reminds us of the account of Moses' call. The prophet understands himself to be a messenger who is summoned and sent, who speaks not his own opinions but the message of his Lord. Hence the frequent messenger formula: "Thus saith the Lord" (see Genesis 32:3–5 for the secular use of

[2] For a full discussion of Jeremiah and his times, see my *Understanding the Old Testament*, 2nd edition (Prentice-Hall, 1966), chapter 11. See also *Rediscovering the Bible*, chapter 5.

the messenger form of speech). Verse 10 is important. Notice that the first effect of God's Word, spoken through his messenger, is destructive; it "roots up and pulls down." Only after this negative or critical function has been performed does it "build and plant." This calls our attention to a characteristic emphasis of the prophetic message: to know God, or rather to be known by him, is to be exposed to his judgment. God sets his plumb line against the unjust structures of society (Amos 7:7–9) and searches the innermost motives of the heart (Psalm 139:1–6). There is no dark corner where the searchlight of his criticism does not reach.

The second passage (Jeremiah 2:1–13), which contains the message of the prophetic messenger (note the messenger formula in 2:1–2 and 2:4–5a), belongs to a literary genre known as the "covenant lawsuit." [3] The prophet, acting as a prosecuting lawyer representing God's Court, reviews the history of Israel in the light of the covenant commitment. Viewed from this standpoint it is a long history of ingratitude and unfaithfulness to the God who had graciously delivered his people from bondage and brought them into a good land. The past is reviewed not for its own sake, but to understand the meaning of the present. Men have

[3] The covenant lawsuit is indicated by the Hebrew verb in verse 9 translated "contend." This literary genre is discussed by Delbert Hillers, *Covenant: The History of a Biblical Idea* (Johns Hopkins Press, 1969), chapter 6.

preferred to live on their own terms, following the idols and the desires of their own hearts. The indictment comes to a resounding climax in verse 13, where the prophet accuses the people of rejecting Him who is "the fountain of living waters" to hew out for themselves "broken cisterns that can hold no water." This is reminiscent of the theme which we have met previously in the Adam story.

The third passage (Jeremiah 7:1–15) comes down to cases more specifically. Jeremiah's Temple sermon, which Jesus later referred to (Mark 11:17), is a bold criticism of religion—that is, the kind of religion which is the tool of the status quo and the justification of accepted values or priorities. The prophet warns the people against supposing that they are safe if they go to church, while their society violates the human dignity of persons and thereby shouts defiance at the sovereignty of God. The ancient shrine of the old tribal confederacy, once located at Shiloh (I Samuel 1:3), had been destroyed without trace by the Philistines; and the same fate would befall the proud temple of Jerusalem. For God is the critic, not the defender, of the social order. He enters into controversy with his people on the basis of the covenant.

■ **Judgment in History**

Jeremiah's message, then, was that God was confronting his people in that historical crisis and was using the Babylonian invader to accomplish his purpose of judgment and discipline. In some respects, his message was like that of Isaiah who, in the latter part of the eighth century B.C., boldly described the Assyrian as "the rod of the Lord's anger" (Isaiah 10:5–19).[4] Men are free to choose their course of action, but they are not free to escape the consequences of those actions as long as God is actively involved in history to accomplish his purpose. He acts to overthrow systems of exploitation, to humble the proud and exalt those of low degree, and to shatter the false gods in which men place their trust. There is, according to the Cambridge historian Herbert Butterfield, a discernible element of judgment in history.[5] But the end of this shock treatment is that men may be brought to their senses, may become more fully human in their relationships, and at last may find their true community in a New Covenant with God. This is the theme of the final passage (Jeremiah 31:31–34) from which the New Testament takes it name.[6]

[4] During the period of Nazi ascendancy in Europe, Harry Emerson Fosdick delivered a hard-hitting sermon on the text from Isaiah, under the title "God Talks to a Dictator." *Living Under Tension: Sermons on Christianity Today* (Harper, 1941), pp. 172–181.

[5] Herbert Butterfield, *Christianity and History* (Charles Scribner's Sons, 1950).

[6] See my exposition of this passage, "The New Covenant and the Old," in *The Old Testament and Christian Faith* (Harper and Row, 1963), pp. 225–242.

Questions to Think About

1. Karl Marx observed that the beginning of all criticism is the criticism of religion. Jeremiah, though speaking from the standpoint of faith in God, would have agreed. Why?

2. Make a list of some of the "broken cisterns" in which modern men have placed their trust. Would you include education, science, psychology, progress, communism, "the American way," organized religion?

3. In his Second Inaugural, Abraham Lincoln said: "If God will that it [the Civil War] continue until every drop of blood drawn by the taskmaster's lash shall be repaid with two drawn by the sword . . . then . . . 'the judgments of the Lord are true and righteous altogether.' " Does our present historical crisis disclose the judgment of God? How should this view affect our attitude as citizens?

4. Discuss the widely held view that religion belongs in one sphere and political and economic issues in another. Would Jeremiah have agreed with the policy of keeping social issues out of the pulpit?

5. Jeremiah believed that God was working through an unbeliever, Nebuchadnezzar, to accomplish his purpose in history. What do you think Jeremiah's attitude would have been today toward the atheistic rulers of the Kremlin? toward radical secular forces of revolution in our society?

6. Suppose that Western civilization should fall, as the Roman Empire collapsed in the time of Augustine. How would a biblical prophet interpret this disaster?

Suggestions for Further Reading

Anderson, Bernhard W., *Understanding the Old Testament,* 2nd ed. (Prentice-Hall, 1966), chapters 7, 8, 9, and especially 11. These chapters discuss in detail the prophetic movement in historical context.

Bright, John, *Jeremiah,* Anchor Bible (Doubleday, 1965). A fresh translation with helpful introduction and notes.

Clements, R. E., *Prophecy and Covenant* (SCM Press, 1966). A valuable discussion of the stance of the prophets in covenant traditions.

von Rad, Gerhard, *The Message of the Prophets* (SCM Press, 1968). Most of this is excerpted from the author's monumental work on *Old Testament Theology,* Vol. II (1965).

Scott, R. B. Y., *The Relevance of the Prophets,* rev. ed. (Macmillan, 1968). One of the best general introductions to the prophets of Israel.

THE NEW EXODUS

STUDY PASSAGES:

We come now to the second main phase of the biblical drama. The scene opens in Babylonia, to which country Judahites or Jews [1] had been deported during the capture of the city of Jerusalem. Many of these displaced persons had settled down in relative prosperity and security in the foreign land, but the vision of Jerusalem, destroyed and impoverished, could not be erased from their memories (see Psalm 137). To them the terrible thing was not just the physical calamity but the religious despair and disillusionment which the fall of Jerusalem had occasioned. For Jerusalem was not an ordinary city to them; it was a center of historical meaning—meaning which had been disclosed by God when he delivered the Israelites from Egypt and providentially guided their history to its greatest fulfillment in the establishment of the dynasty of David.

■ A Spiritual Blackout

The crisis of the fall of Jerusalem was experienced intensely by the people of the Southern Kingdom (Judah) who shared the covenant theology associated with King David (see Study III). Southern interpreters of Israel's tradition maintained

[1] While "Israel" refers to the whole People of God, "Jew" originally designated the residents of the southern kingdom of Judah (*i.e.*, Judahites) who were exiled from their land. "Samaritans," on the other hand, were the former citizens of the Northern Kingdom (Samaria) who previously had been exiled by the Assyrians.

that the climax of God's saving activity with Israel was his choice of David as king and his choice of Zion (Jerusalem) as the sacramental place of his presence (Psalms 78; 132). It was their conviction that God had bound himself graciously to David and his line with an unconditional oath and that he had set aside Jerusalem as the "City of God" (see Psalms 46, 84). This theology was a guarantee of social stability amid the disorders of history, where every change of administration was an opportunity for disruptive, chaotic forces to break loose.[2] Yet the poignant question arose: If God had bound himself to David with promises of grace and to Jerusalem as the place where Israel should worship him, why did he allow a calamity to take place which brought the Davidic line to an end and destroyed the Temple? The anguish of those who shared these convictions is vividly expressed in the lament found in Psalm 89 (especially verses 38–51).

The fall of Jerusalem was thus a spiritual blackout, especially for those who identified God's purpose in history with the preservation of the Davidic state. Jeremiah 28 provides a vivid description of the tension between nationalism and faith, between popular prophecy and true prophecy. The popular prophet had declared: "God is

[2] See my discussion of the theology of social stability represented by the Davidic covenant in *Creation versus Chaos* (Association Press, 1967), chapter 2, "Creation and Covenant." Also G. Ernest Wright, *The Old Testament and Theology* (Harper and Row, 1969), chapter 3.

with us" (the meaning of the Hebrew word *Immanuel*), therefore no evil can come upon us. The true prophet had said, "God is with us," therefore all securities—Jerusalem, the Temple, organized religion, the nation—stand under his judgment. It is easy to see how those who had been beguiled by popular prophecy would have concluded that God had "let them down" when Jerusalem was destroyed. It seemed that God's history with his people was a history of failure.

However, the God who performed the miracle of the Exodus was about to make himself known in another mighty act of deliverance. This is the testimony of a series of magnificent poems found in the latter part of the Book of Isaiah (chapters 40–55). Speaking to despairing exiles in Babylonia, this prophet announces the good news that the God of Israel, who controls the destinies of all nations, will accomplish the return of the Israelites to their homeland where they would take their part in the fulfillment of the divine purpose for history. Strikingly, this prophet resorts to the imagery of the exodus from Egypt to describe Israel's new "going out" from captivity and the opening of a new way into the future (Isaiah 44:27; 43:16f.; 51:10f.; and compare Exodus 14:15–31). It is appropriate, then, to speak of this event as the "New Exodus." [3]

[3] The motif of the "New Exodus" I have discussed at greater length in "Exodus Typology in Second Isaiah," in *Israel's Prophetic Heritage,* edited by B. W. Anderson and Walter Harrelson (Harper and Row, 1962), pp. 177-195.

■ The All-embracing Purpose of God

It is generally recognized that the last part of the present Book of Isaiah, particularly chapters 40 through 55, comes from the pen of an unknown prophet who lived during the period of the Exile.[4] In his time the Babylonian empire was declining, and the political news on the international scene was the rise of a ruler named Cyrus (Isaiah 44:28; 45:1). Having established control over the Medes and the Persians (about 550 B.C.), Cyrus marched into the heart of the Babylonian empire and in 538 Babylon fell. The "Second Isaiah" was active in the period between the rise of the new conqueror and the final capitulation of Babylon— that is, between 550 and 538 B.C. An enlightened monarch, Cyrus' policy was that of granting captive peoples the right to live in their own countries and to carry on their own traditions. Small wonder that many people, who groaned under the heavy yoke of Babylonia, looked to him as a messianic liberator! This is the life situation to which the Unknown Prophet spoke. His task as a prophetic messenger was not just to predict the imminent downfall of Babylon and the release of captives, but to interpret the religious meaning of this momentous event.

The best way to prepare for this study is to read

[4] The Unknown Prophet of the Exile is usually called the Second Isaiah to distinguish him from the earlier Isaiah of Jerusalem (740–700 B.C.) whose prophecies are found in the first section of the Book of Isaiah.

through all fifteen chapters of Second Isaiah
(Isaiah 40–55) in a modern translation. Even
from a purely literary point of view this is poetry
at its finest; and from a theological viewpoint these
poems represent the crowning maturity of the faith
of Israel. The passages selected set forth themes
which are elaborated with symphonic splendor in
the prophet's work as a whole. The central thrust
of the prophetic message is that world events do
not happen by caprice, but are embraced within
the overruling sovereignty of God, the Creator
and Redeemer, to whom Israel's historical traditions bear witness.

▪ A Herald of Good News

Like a prologue, the first passage (Isaiah 40:1–
11) sets the tone of the whole series of poems.
The prophet (who appears in the "I" of verse 6)
feels that he has stood, as it were, within the
Heavenly Council where God was heard issuing a
decree to be announced to Israel—and to the
whole world. A key word in this section is "good
news" (verse 9; cf. 52:7), the word which re-
appears in the New Testament as "gospel." What
is the content of this good news? It is this: God is
about to act, just as at the beginning of Israel's
history he had taken the initiative in delivering
a people from a no-exit situation and opening a
way through the wilderness to a promised future.
To an unbeliever, perhaps, there would be nothing
extraordinary in the return of exiles to their home-

land; but to those who viewed this event in the perspective of the Exodus and the whole Israelite tradition this would be a theophany—that is, a manifestation of the glory of God on the stage of history. "See, the Lord God is coming with might," like a shepherd who leads and cares for his flock (verses 10–11; cf. 52:7–10). In the prophet's ecstatic faith, the historical drama was moving toward the dawn of the New Age, the Kingdom of God. It is significant that at the beginning of the third stage of the biblical drama John the Baptist recapitulates the theme of this chapter (compare Isaiah 40:3 with Mark 1:3).

One of the central themes of the prophet's message is the *novelty* of God's action in history (Isaiah 42:5–17 and 43:14–21). Life is lived not merely within the order of nature with its recurring rhythms of "seedtime and harvest, cold and heat, summer and winter, day and night" (Genesis 8:22), but is caught up in a purposive movement of historical events that are new, unique, and unrepeatable. The nations, when brought to trial, are unable to testify to this divine purpose in which the startling developments under Cyrus are related to "the former things" (the call of Abraham, the Exodus from Egypt, the march through the wilderness to the Promised Land). But Israel, out of her own life story, bears witness to the God whose purpose spans the ages, from beginning to end.

At times the prophet seems to stress the newness

of God's action so sharply that the past is to be forgotten:

> Remember not the former things,
>   nor consider the things of old.
> Behold, I am doing a new thing;
>   now it springs forth, do you not perceive it?
>   —Isaiah 43:18–19

Yet the prophet is equally insistent that Israel should "remember the former things of old" (Isaiah 46:8–11). These statements are not contradictory when one considers the creative manner in which the prophet reinterprets the old traditions so that they are convincingly relevant to the present situation in which the community finds itself. Here the Israelite tradition is not just a past memory but provides the imagery for understanding the new thing which God is doing, the new word which he is speaking. Again and again the prophet resorts to the tradition of the Exodus from Egypt to describe the New Exodus of Salvation. He is not talking, however, about a repetition of the first Exodus; rather, the imagery of the old is used poetically to express the divine surprise in the present.

■ The Servant of the Lord

According to Second Isaiah, Israel is the Lord's "Servant" (Isaiah 41:8–10; 43:8–13; 44:1–2). This Servant is blind, deaf, and stubborn; nevertheless, despite his weaknesses, he has been chosen for a unique role in the accomplishment of God's historical purpose. God had an ulterior motive in delivering Israel from Babylonian bondage; namely, that Israel might be "a light to the nations" (42:6; cf. 49:6). Here the prophet understands profoundly the meaning of the call of Abraham to be a blessing to the families of the earth (Genesis 12:1–3).

This theme is developed with sublime grandeur in our third passage (Isaiah 52:12–53:13) which belongs to a series of special "servant poems." [5] In this passage, one of the most important in the whole Old Testament, the "Suffering Servant" is portrayed in the guise of an individual. At the beginning and end of the poem (52:13–15 and 53:10–13) God speaks, announcing the exaltation of his Servant. In the central portion (53:1–9) the spokesmen for the nations testify. They have come to realize that the meaning of Israel's suffering was not merely that the people had experienced the discipline of divine judgment. That was part of the matter, to be sure, but there was a much deeper truth. The Servant's suffering was vicarious —that is, it was borne for others. Through the Servant's affliction the peoples were made whole, restored to health, "justified" or brought into right relationship with God and with one another. This is the most astounding testimony of the Bible:

[5] Besides this chapter, there are three other Servant poems: Isaiah 42:1–4; 49:1–6; 50:4–9. The identity of the Servant in Second Isaiah is a moot question. See my discussion in *Understanding the Old Testament,* 2nd edition (Prentice-Hall, 1966), pp. 414–427.

that God chooses the way of humiliation, suffering, rejection, and defeat to make known his victory and sovereignty in the world. And this is the truth which is fulfilled and "made flesh" in the New Testament.

■ The Promises of Grace

The final chapter (Isaiah 55:1–13) rounds off the prophet's message by sounding again the theme of unconditional pardon and grace heard at the beginning. A free-for-all invitation is given to God's banquet table. Here the startling announcement is made that the unconditional covenant of grace, once made with David according to royal theology (II Samuel 7), is now extended to *the people* (Isaiah 55:3). The covenant relation with God is not based upon obedience to legal stipulations, as in the Mosaic covenant, but is grounded solely upon the grace of God whose thoughts are not our thoughts and whose ways are not our ways. God makes an "everlasting covenant" with his people, like the covenant with Noah whose sign is the bow in the clouds (54:9–10; cf. Genesis 9:8–17). This covenant of grace, which is central to the gospel of the New Testament, does not relieve men from responsibility. Rather, it brings man's service to God under a rainbow of divine purpose which, at one end, is lost in the beginning of creation and, at the other, fades into the horizon of the consummation of the whole drama of history and creation.

Questions to Think About

1. Contrast Second Isaiah's understanding of history with the nihilistic view that history has no ultimate meaning and that we must find our temporary meanings. What is the ground for saying that all human history is embraced within a single purpose, from beginning to end?

2. How does the prophet's announcement that God is "doing a new thing" speak to our time? Does this demand a break with past tradition and a radically new theology?

3. Compare the Mosaic covenant and its conditional stipulations with the "everlasting convenant" which is grounded solely in divine grace. Do you think that a greater emphasis upon divine grace (pardon, forgiveness) undercuts the motive for human action and responsibility?

4. How does Second Isaiah view the "election" or call of Israel as having a special role in the divine purpose? How do you account for "the mystery of Israel"—the people which has survived through the centuries to the present?

5. Granting that the Church is the "New Israel," does it participate with Jesus Christ in the mystery of the Suffering Servant? If so, what does it mean to share the fellowship of Christ's sufferings?

Suggestions for Further Reading

Anderson, Bernhard W., *Understanding the Old Testament*, 2nd ed. (Prentice-Hall, 1966), chapter 13.

McKenzie, John, *Second Isaiah*, Anchor Bible (Doubleday, 1968). A fresh translation with helpful introduction and notes by a Roman Catholic scholar.

Muilenburg, James, "Introduction to and Exegesis of Second Isaiah," in the *Interpreter's Bible*, Vol. V (Abingdon, 1956). One of the best commentaries on Second Isaiah.

Westermann, Claus, *Isaiah 40–66,* Old Testament Library Series (Westminster, 1969). An excellent commentary by a leading German scholar.

THE PEOPLE OF THE TORAH

STUDY PASSAGES:

1. Nehemiah 8 and 9
   The Renewal of the Covenant

2. Psalm 1 and Psalm 19:7–14
   Rejoicing in the Torah

3. Psalms 37 and 73
   Wisdom Psalms

4. The Book of Job
   (at least the following):
   Prose prologue (1:1–2:13)
   Job's lament (chapter 3)

Parts of the first cycle of speeches
 (chapters 4–14)
Job's final defense
 (especially chapter 31)
The Voice from the Whirlwind
 (chapter 38)
Job's repentance (42:1–6)

This brings us to one of the most important, though for many Christians the most problematic, phases of the biblical drama. The spotlight falls on Ezra and Nehemiah, two men who played a decisive role in the re-formation of Israel into the community known as Judaism.[1] Someone has said that Israel went into exile as a nation and returned as a church. The word *Judaism* refers to a new stage in the biblical drama when *Israel* was no longer a state but a religious community—somewhat analogous to the time before David when the people were united in a tribal confederacy on the basis of covenant allegiance. This worshipping community was an ellipse with two centers: the Temple and the Torah.

[1] The religious phenomenon called Judaism emerged during the period after the Exile when "Jews" (former residents of Judah) returned to Palestine. It was characterized by devotion to the Mosaic Torah (the Pentateuch) as the constitutional basis of life and thought.

■ A New Beginning

To see this in proper perspective, let's resume the story from the time of Second Isaiah, practically a century earlier than the period of Ezra. Shortly after Babylon capitulated to the Persian army, Cyrus issued an edict allowing Jews the privilege of returning to their homeland. So Jewish exiles began their homeward trek to Zion (Jerusalem). When they arrived, they found everything in ruins: the Temple was destroyed, the walls of Jerusalem were leveled, the city desolate. Nevertheless, inspired by the prophecies of Haggai and Zechariah, they set about rebuilding the Temple, a project which was completed about 515 B.C.

Then Ezra came onto the scene, according to the sequence of events given by the historian who wrote the Books of Chronicles, Ezra, and Nehemiah. With the permission of the Persian king he led a caravan of Jews back to Palestine around the middle of the fifth century B.C. (or slightly later). Most important, he brought with him a copy of "the book of the Law [Torah] of Moses," [2] and he lost no time in convening the people to hear the reading of its contents. One of the solemn moments in Israel's history is described in Nehemiah 8 and 9, a great occasion of covenant renewal. The ceremony included the public reading of the Torah to the people, the offering of a

[2] This book probably contained essentially the Pentateuch, the so-called Five Books of Moses.

penitential prayer which summarized the Lord's gracious dealings with his people throughout their historical pilgrimage, and the covenant pledge of the people "to walk in God's law [torah], which was given by Moses the servant of God." The event is to be compared with the covenant-renewal ceremony led by Joshua (Joshua 24) or by King Josiah (II Kings 23).

At about the same time Nehemiah, a cupbearer to the Persian king, received permission to return to Palestine as a Persian governor of Judah. After a memorable midnight tour around the city walls of Jerusalem, he organized the Jews for work and in less than two months the walls were rebuilt, despite hostile resistance. Thus under the religious leadership of Ezra and the statesmanship of Nehemiah the "congregation of Israel" took a new lease on life. It seemed as though the glowing promises spoken by prophets like Second Isaiah were on the verge of fulfillment.[3]

■ **Covenant Renewal**

The vitality of Judaism is indicated by the great amount of biblical literature which comes from the period following the Exile. The Pentateuch (the first five books of the Old Testament) received its final form in this period. Indeed, the whole Old Testament as we have received it is stamped in-

[3] For a discussion of these developments, see *Understanding the Old Testament,* 2nd edition (Prentice-Hall, 1966), chapter 14, "A Kingdom of Priests."

delibly with the way of life and thought characteristic of the time. In this study we can do little more than scratch the surface of biblical Judaism, the stage of Israel's historical pilgrimage out of which Christianty emerged in the fullness of time.

The best way to prepare for this study is to familiarize yourself with the account of Ezra's career as related in the following chapters: Ezra 7–8; Nehemiah 8–10; Ezra 9–10 (the chapters should be read in that order). In these chapters you will find an emphasis upon ritual, or "priestly," matters which loom large in long sections of the Pentateuch, as well as the concern for maintaining the purity of the faith by rigid laws against mixed marriages. Above all, you should give attention to the account of Ezra's reading of the Torah (Nehemiah 8:1–8) and the solemn liturgical prayer which followed (Nehemiah 9:6–38).

Notice that the prayer strikes a note characteristic of Israel's faith from the first. It is a summary of "the mighty acts of the Lord" by which Israel had been brought onto the stage of history with a unique vocation and destiny. Penitently the people acknowledge that the Exile was God's judgment upon their covenant unfaithfulness; gratefully they rejoice in the New Exodus from Babylonian captivity; solemnly they vow to renew the covenant by obeying the stipulations of the Torah. This is one of the great confessions of faith in the Old Testament. Unlike Israel's early creedal confession (Deuteronomy 26:5–9), the recital of

God's saving acts begins with the creation, as does the "salvation history" Psalm 136 which probably comes from this period. We have already found this spacious perspective in the message of Second Isaiah, which was addressed to "the people in whose heart is my [God's] law" (Isaiah 51:7). And in the portrayal of the Consummation found in Isaiah 2:1–5 (Micah 4:1–4) the peoples of the world stream to Jerusalem from which God's torah, or word, goes forth. Thus the Torah discloses the meaning of all history and creation.

■ Rejoicing in the Torah

Of the great amount of literature from the period of Judaism we have selected some of the psalms of Israel and some of the writings from Israel's wisdom movement for special study. The Book of Psalms is so important in Jewish and Christian worship that it would call for a special study by itself.[4] Like modern hymnbooks, it reflects a long history of worship in which songs of various types are included: hymns of praise (*e.g.,* Psalm 103), laments and confessions of sin (Psalms 22, 51), thanksgivings (Psalm 118), and songs for use on special occasions (Psalm 47, a New Year's psalm). The final edition of the Book of Psalms, however, is a product of the period of Judaism and is ap-

---

[4] See my study book, *Out of the Depths: The Psalms Speak to Us Today* (Service Center, Board of Missions, United Methodist Church, Cincinnati, Ohio, 1970). See especially chapter 7.

propriately arranged in five books like the Pentateuch itself. The hymnbook is introduced with two
psalms which set forth the cardinal tenets of
Judaism: Psalm 1, which glorifies the study of
God's Torah (see also Psalm 19:7–14), and
Psalm 2 which in this period, as in the time of the
New Testament, was understood to refer to the
Messiah (see also Psalm 110). Thus these introductory psalms invite readers "to choose the right
path to the Messianic glory: the study of the law
and obedience toward the word of God." [5]

So, after familiarizing yourself with the Ezra
story, turn to Psalm 1. This psalm draws a distinc-
tion between two kinds of persons: the "God-
fearer" who delights in God's Torah day and night
and who therefore is like a tree whose roots are
nourished by life-giving waters; and the "wicked"
person or the "fool" (Psalm 14:1) who vainly
lives by his own standards, without dependence
upon God. Remember that when the Israelite
thought of God's "Law," he did not think of a
Heavenly Policeman who coldly enforces statutes;
rather, he confessed his relationship to the God
who had graciously redeemed Israel from bondage
and had given them "teaching" or "direction" (the
proper translation of the Hebrew word *torah*) in
the way they should walk. From the very first the
Covenant and the Torah were linked together. As
time went on, many "laws" were added to the
covenant tradition, and under Ezra the Torah was

[5] Aage Bentzen, *Introduction to the Old Testament*,
Vol. II, 4th ed. (G.E.C. Gads Vorlag, 1958), p. 170.

identified especially with the Pentateuch, the so-called Five Books of Moses. You would think that obeying the many instructions of this Torah would be burdensome. But reading the Torah psalms (Psalms 1; 19:7–14; 119) will disclose that Judaism found God's Torah a delight, "rejoicing the heart" (Psalm 19:8). For the chief concern was that of glorifying God in all daily actions and relationships.

■ The Beginning of Wisdom

Ezra's great reform had its strengths, but also had great dangers which were evident to those who reflected deeply upon the sufferings and imbalances of life.[6] It is one thing to delight in God's will; it is another thing to be so self-righteously sure of what God's will is in a specific situation that men thank God that they are not as other people (see the parable of the Pharisee and the publican, Luke 18:9–14). Perhaps modern churches and synagogues fall into this danger insofar as a middle-class code of "thou shalts" and "thou shalt nots" is set forth as the standard of virtue. And leaders who claim that God is on our side in the international struggle imply self-righteously that our enemies are the wicked who fall short of the glory of God. According to the prophets, God's will brought his people under judgment; the Lord had

[6] See *Rediscovering the Bible*, chapter 6, especially pp. 137–143.

a controversy with Israel. If you think seriously about how impossible it is to stand before God on the basis of our moral goodness (Psalm 130:3), perhaps you can anticipate why the Christian Gospel protests against all legalism and moralism and puts man's relation with God on an entirely different basis from the Torah, or "Law" (Galatians 2:11–21).

The belief of Judaism was that God's Torah is the source of wisdom, as we can see from a wisdom psalm like Psalm 37 (see especially verses 30–31). Wisdom, therefore, is not a human achievement but a gift bestowed by God, one that inspires humility and reverence.

> Behold, the fear of the Lord, that is wisdom;
> and to depart from evil is understanding.
> —Job 28:28

In Israel's wisdom circle there was deep searching into the mystery of human existence and the marvelous order of nature, and hence a dissatisfaction with simple solutions to life's problems. Even the sharp line between the righteous and the wicked, the God-fearer and the God-scoffer (as delineated in Psalm 1) was called into question.

■ **The Voice from the Whirlwind**

The greatest literary contribution from the wisdom circle came from the writer of the Book of Job. This writer has aptly been acclaimed as "the Shakespeare of the Old Testament." Here we can only touch on this powerful outpouring of the human spirit in the face of life's baffling mystery.[7] An old folk tale, written in prose, now stands as the prologue and epilogue to a poetic work consisting of Job's lament, his conversation with his friends in three rounds, his final oath of innocence, God's answer out of the whirlwind, and Job's final repentance. (The Elihu speech in chapters 32–37 seems to be a later addition to the poem of Job.) The Job of the folk tale was a traditional righteous man, "blameless and upright, one who feared God, and turned away from evil"—a man who bore adversity with calm patience and who was long-suffering. The Job of the poem, however, refuses to suffer "the slings and arrows of outrageous fortune" meekly and without protest. Not only does he challenge his three orthodox friends, who steadfastly insist that his suffering has been brought about by some sin, but he dares to accuse God of maladministration of justice on earth. Finally, after an overwhelming demonstration of God's wisdom and power as Creator (the Voice from the Whirlwind), Job acknowledges that he has no ground on which to challenge the Almighty and repents of his presumptuous speech.

Probably in this study unit you should concentrate on the Book of Job. What is the real problem with which Job wrestles? Why cannot he accept

---

[7] For further discussion of the Book of Job see especially Samuel Terrien, *Job, Poet of Existence* (Bobbs-Merrill, 1958). Other readings are suggested at the end of this study unit.

the "pastoral counseling" of his friends? Is the Voice from the Whirlwind an answer to Job's question? Why does Job repent or recant in the end? Doubtless you will find that this poetry penetrates the deepest levels of human existence and provides a good context for appropriating the meaning of the Gospel of the New Testament.

QUESTIONS TO THINK ABOUT

1. The first Psalm suggests that the person who obeys the will of God will enjoy security, influence, and long life. Discuss the difference between the attitude of this psalm and that of Psalm 73 with its great "nevertheless" in verse 23.

2. What strengths and weaknesses do you see in Ezra's great reform? Discuss what "legalism" means in the Church today.

3. The great keynote of Israel's sages was: "The fear of the Lord is the beginning of wisdom" (Proverbs 9:10; 15:33; Job 28:28; Psalm 111:10). Consider what this means, perhaps by studying the magnificent poem in Job 28.

4. Archibald Macleish has attempted to interpret the meaning of the Book of Job for our time in his play *J.B.: A Play in Verse* (Riverside Press, Sentry Edition, 1961). What aspects of the poem of Job does he ignore? What new dimensions are added?

5. The test of any religion is how it deals with the problem of suffering and evil. How is this problem dealt with in the prophecy represented by Jeremiah? in Second Isaiah's portrayal of the Suffering Servant? in the Book of Job?

Suggestions for Further Reading

Anderson, Bernhard W., *Understanding the Old Testament,* 2nd ed. (Prentice-Hall, 1966), chapters 14, 15, 16 (on Job: pp. 506–518).

Kelly, Balmer H., *Ezra to Job,* Layman's Bible Commentary (John Knox Press, 1962).

Paterson, John, *The Wisdom of Israel,* Bible Guides (Lutterworth, Abingdon, 1961). A good, brief introduction to wisdom literature.

Snaith, Norman H., *The Book of Job: Its Origin and Purpose,* Studies in Biblical Theology, Second Series, Vol. 11 (Alec R. Allenson, 1968). A fresh approach to the literary unity of the Book of Job, it argues that the main problem is how the transcendent God can be related to the world of human affairs.

Terrien, Samuel, "Introduction to and Exegesis of the Book of Job," in *The Interpreter's Bible,* Vol. III (Abingdon, 1954). A perceptive, scholarly interpretation. See also his *Job: Poet of Existence* (Bobbs-Merrill, 1958).

VICTORY THROUGH DEFEAT

STUDY PASSAGES:

The historical drama, in which God is the Chief Actor, has now reached its climax. The New Testament opens with the exuberant announcement that God's promises to Israel are being fulfilled. John the Baptist, the last of Israel's prophets before the dawn of the Messianic Age, appears on the scene in a manner reminiscent of Elijah, announcing that the great Consummation (the Day of Judgment and Renewal) is at hand. Jesus of Nazareth steps onto the stage of history at this crucial juncture and his message is pitched to a key of urgency: "The time is fulfilled, and the kingdom of God is at hand; repent, and believe in the gospel" (Mark 1:15).

■ The Christian Good News

In Study IV it was pointed out that the Christian term "gospel" has its scriptural background in passages of Second Isaiah where the prophet, like a herald, announced the good news of God's coming in triumph to inaugurate his Kingdom (Isaiah 52:7–10). Likewise in the New Testament the Gospel is the Good News that God's Redemptive Rule (Kingdom) has begun, that the new age has dawned. The Good News is not a new doctrine, such as the Fatherhood of God and the brotherhood of man (cf. Malachi 2:10), but is the announcement of what God *does;* his action to deliver men from the bondage of evil, darkness, and death, and his re-creation of human life with new possibilities of freedom and fulfillment. Moreover, the New Testament proclaims that the Good News is Jesus himself—his words and works which confront men with the authority of one who is uniquely *anointed* to be God's agent.[1] Jesus preaches with eschatological urgency: *now* is the time to decide, tomorrow may be too late; for the Kingdom of God is at hand![2] Above all, the Gospel focuses on the Crucifixion and, the other side of this event, the Resurrection. If the Exodus was a mighty act of God, if the deliverance of Jewish exiles from captivity was a divine deed, then God's greatest miracle in history was what has been called the "Christ Event"—the whole life, death, and resurrection of Jesus and the consequent emergence of the Church.[3]

The written Gospels (Matthew, Mark, Luke, John) are not biographies in our sense of the word but are primarily confessions of faith, each with a different accent and concern. This does not mean that the literary Gospels belong in the category of fiction or fantasy, for the gospel story is based securely upon the earthly career of a historical person. Nevertheless, Jesus' words and

[1] The Greek word for Christ (*Christos*) is equivalent to the Hebrew word for Messiah (*Mashiach*) which means "Anointed One"—that is, one who is consecrated as the agent of God's rule.

[2] "Eschatological" comes from a Greek word *eschata* referring to "the last things"—that is, the End. In this context "End" refers to the great Consummation which is so near that it is already beginning to break into history.

[3] See John Knox, *On the Meaning of Christ* (Charles Scribner's Sons, 1947). A fuller discussion of this study unit is found in my *Rediscovering the Bible,* chapters 7–9.

works were remembered in the experience of those who, after the Crucifixion and Resurrection, were convinced that he was God's Messiah (Christ). Thus in the earliest Gospel, Mark, the whole focus of interest is the Passion of Christ. Another formulation of the Christian gospel is found in Peter's sermon as presented in Acts 10:34–43, a passage which you should take time to read, for it presents the basic outline of the Christian story.

■ The Denouement of the Historical Drama

To appreciate the Christian conviction that the Christ Event is the fulfillment and climax of the previous episodes of the biblical drama, let's take a brief glance back at the story which has unfolded thus far. The biblical drama begins by describing in pictorial terms man's estrangement from God: the misuse of man's God-given freedom and the resulting confusion, conflict, and chaos in history. To deal with this general human predicament, God took the initiative—so we are told in Genesis 12:1–3—and called Abraham, promising him that he and his descendants would be a blessing to the broken and distraught families of mankind. So "Israel" was called and formed as a special community in order that this People might be the bearer of God's purpose in history, the agent for the accomplishment of his historical plan. Israel's record, however, was one of persistent betrayal of the covenant loyalty, and the catastrophes that struck in the periods of Assyrian and Babylonian world rule were interpreted by prophets as the discipline of God's judgment. Then, buoyed by the stirring prophecy of Second Isaiah and the leadership of Ezra and Nehemiah, a fresh start was made after the Exile. But, in the period of Judaism, Israel became so preoccupied with the problem of preserving her own identity and tradition that the world mission described by Second Isaiah was almost lost to sight, except for a few witnesses like the Book of Jonah. At last, in the fullness of time (Galatians 4:4), Jesus of Nazareth appeared in the context of the history of God's People.

Then came, at a predetermined moment, a moment in time and of time,
A moment not out of time, but in time, in what we call history;
transecting, bisecting the world of time, a moment in time but not like a moment of time,
A moment in time but time was made through that moment;
for without the meaning there is no time, and that moment of time gave the meaning.[4]

Thus the Christian Church affirms that in this "moment of time," which divides history into B.C. and A.D., God has made a new beginning, has introduced the New Age in which men may begin to experience a richer and fuller humanity. Through

[4] T. S. Eliot, from Choruses from *The Rock*, VII, *Collected Poems 1909–1935* (Harcourt, Brace, and Co., 1936), p. 199. Used by permission.

Christ, the Church proclaims, a new life is available: a new relation to God and, as a corollary, a new relation between human beings. Jeremiah's prophecy of the New Covenant (see Study III) took on deeper meaning for Christians who appropriated the scriptural tradition. The Christian community, like the monastic community which flourished at Qumran on the shore of the Dead Sea,[5] understood itself to be the community of the New Covenant. When the shadow of the Cross fell upon the table at the Last Supper, Jesus said to his disciples, "This cup is the new covenant in my blood" (I Corinthians 11:25; cf. Luke 22:20), recalling both the ceremony at Sinai (Exodus 24:3–8) and Jeremiah's prophecy (Jeremiah 31:31–34).

■ The New Christian Language

The Christian community, however, did not merely repeat the tradition of the past but used it creatively to declare what God is doing now. Perhaps the major characteristic of this community was the new language that it used to tell the Christian gospel. The "narrative mode," Amos Wilder points out, "is uniquely important to Christianity," unlike other religions and philosophies in which

---

[5] The Essene community of Qumran thought of itself as the eschatological community of the New Covenant. See Charles T. Fritsch, *The Qumran Community* (Macmillan, 1956); Helmer Ringgren, *The Faith of Qumran* (Fortress Press, 1961).

in the drama. The recurring question is: Who is this Stranger who speaks with authority, who performs the deeds which evidence God's active presence in the world, who is rejected by the religious authorities and misunderstood by his own followers, and who finally goes his lonely way to the cross? "Who do *you* say that I am?" Neutrality is out of the question; decision is demanded.

Notice that the mystery of Jesus' identity was heightened by his announcement to his disciples that his vocation was that of the Suffering Servant and that those who follow after him would share his suffering. Strangely, he *must* suffer. Why this divine necessity? In those days it was generally believed that the Messiah would come triumphantly to restore the lost fortunes of Israel, either by political action or supernatural power, and achieve thereby a victory that would be clear to all. How incredible that Second Isaiah's portrayal of the Suffering Servant, which the prophet apparently applied to the sufferings of Israel (see Study IV), could be a depiction of the role of the triumphant Messiah!

The story of the Transfiguration (Mark 9:2–13) connects the Crucifixion–Resurrection with the previous episodes of the biblical drama. In Israelite tradition the appearance of a prophet "like Moses" (Deuteronomy 18:15–16) or another Elijah (Malachi 4:5) would mark the time of the End, the coming of God's Kingdom. It is significant, then, that in the disciples' vision these two figures, Moses and Elijah, appear in company with Jesus.

In a kind of religious ecstasy the disciples perceive the splendid uniqueness of Jesus; but the sequel of Mark's story shows that they could not really understand the divine victory that lay on the other side of the Cross. Their continuing lack of faith is a commentary on Jesus' rebuke to Peter for being not on the side of God, but of men (Mark 8:33).

■ The Scandal of the Cross

The theme of the mystery of the Cross is treated at greater length in a letter Paul addressed to the church at the Greek city of Corinth (I Corinthians 1:17–2:13). Here Paul points out that to the non-believer, whether Jew or Gentile, the Cross is either "foolishness" or an "offence, stumbling-block" (*skandalon*). If the Christian gospel were only the preaching of a loftier ethic or the belief in a Supreme Being the world would have little difficulty with this faith. But the trouble is that Christians proclaim the wisdom of God in what men consider foolishness, and the power of God in what men regard as weakness and defeat. Take away the Cross, Paul testifies, and there is no Gospel to proclaim. The Cross is the distinctive Christian symbol of God's victory in apparent defeat. "By this sign conquer."

Some of you may think it strange that we do not focus our attention first on Jesus' teachings as found in the Sermon on the Mount (Matthew 5–7). The reason for this is that the early Christians did not start there. They began, rather, with a recital of the story of Jesus—his Passion and his Resurrection. Teachings and ethical exhortations had their proper place *after* one was drawn into the believing community. As the late D. T. Niles once observed: "The Sermon on the Mount is more a statement of what will happen to a man when he allows Jesus to get hold of him, than a statement of what a man must do if he is to follow Jesus." [7] The Good News was not an ethical code or a new religious idea. It was, rather, the telling of the marvelous story that in the man Jesus, God had actively entered into the human struggle, changing Jesus' suffering and defeat into victory by raising him from the dead and inaugurating a "new creation." Paul discusses the momentous results of God's action in another communication to the church at Corinth which deserves your careful study (II Corinthians 5:14–6:2). There he announces the triumphant theme that "God was in Christ reconciling the world to himself" (II Corinthians 5:19)—overcoming the sin which finds expression in our separation from God, from each other, and from our true selves, and restoring men to the unity and dignity which God intends for his creation.

QUESTIONS TO THINK ABOUT

1. Is there any real significance in the fact that the appearance of Jesus Christ has divided our Western

[7] D. T. Niles, *That They May Have Life* (Harper and Row, 1951), p. 47.

calendar into B.C. and A.D.? Why not start with an assumed date for Creation (as in the Jewish calendar) or perhaps with some dramatic event that marked the opening of the space age?

2. Viewed in the light of the New Testament, how is Jesus' death different from the martyrdom of Socrates, Lincoln, Gandhi, or Martin Luther King? Why was the Cross "necessary" in the accomplishment of God's purpose for mankind?

3. Evaluate the popular view that the essence of Christianity is the Golden Rule or the Sermon on the Mount. What is the "new" that has been introduced through God's action in Jesus Christ?

4. The famous historian Arnold Toynbee once said that the Transfiguration is the key to the Christian interpretation of history. Does it make sense to affirm that the hidden meaning of world history is disclosed in Jesus Christ?

5. Why is the Cross a "scandal" (offence, stumbling-block) to many modern people? Have you become familiar with this "scandalous Cross" or are you more familiar with a watered-down Christianity? Discuss the "costs" of Christian discipleship.

Suggestions for Further Reading

Bornkamm, Günther, *Jesus of Nazareth* (Harper and Row, 1960). An exciting new approach to Jesus, the man and his message.

Kee, Howard, *Jesus in History: An Approach to the Study of the Gospels* (Harcourt, Brace, and World, Inc., 1970), chapter 4. An illuminating treatment of Mark's gospel in the light of "apocalyptic" tradition.

———, Franklin Young and Karlfried Froehlich,

Understanding the New Testament, 2nd ed. (Prentice-Hall, 1965). See especially the chapters dealing with Mark and the Corinthian correspondence (chapters 8, 11).

Lohse, E., *Mark's Witness to Jesus Christ,* World Christian Books (Association Press, 1955). Recommended for the general reader.

Minear, Paul, *The Gospel According to Mark,* Layman's Bible Commentaries (John Knox Press, 1962). Clear, concise introduction.

Nineham, Dennis E., *The Gospel of Saint Mark,* Pelican Gospel Commentaries (Penguin Books, 1964). Text of the Revised Standard Version with valuable commentary.

Wilder, Amos, *The Language of the Gospel* (Harper and Row, 1964). A clearly written, incisive contribution to the understanding of the New Testament.

STUDY VII

THE CHURCH IN THE WORLD

STUDY PASSAGES:

1. Romans 9–11
    The Israel of God

2. I Peter 2:4–10
    The Rejected Stone as the
    Cornerstone

3. Ephesians 1:3 to 2:22
    The Church in God's Universal
    Design

4. John 17
    That They May Be One

In this study our attention focuses on a new emergent in history: the Church of Jesus Christ. From the very first, Christianity was characterized by an *esprit de corps,* a sense of membership in a corporate reality which Paul called "the body of Christ" (I Corinthians 12:27). The individualism which characterizes some modern expressions of Christianity is completely foreign to the New Testament, so much so that the phrase "individual Christian" is a contradiction in terms. The various churches at Antioch, Jerusalem, Ephesus, Corinth and elsewhere were local manifestations of the corporate whole, the Body. Jesus himself conceived his mission to be that of calling the remnant of Israel—twelve disciples, corresponding to the twelve-tribe structure of Israel. And when the meaning of Jesus' life, death, and resurrection came upon these disciples with overwhelming power at the festival of Pentecost (Acts 2), one of the major annual festivals of the Israelite calendar, a great miracle occurred. This small community became a dynamic and militant Church, with a message that "turned the world upside down" (Acts 17:6) and a gospel which was carried enthusiastically to the ends of the earth. The Acts of the Apostles gives the story of the emerging, expanding Church. And every line of the New Testament presupposes the New Community.

■ The Israel of God

While stressing the newness of the Church, we must also keep in mind the relation of this community to the whole Old Testament heritage. In a certain sense the Church may be called "the New Israel." The Old Testament narrates how God chose and formed a People to be the bearer of his purpose in history and the instrument of his saving work. Israel was not a race or a nation, but a covenant community created by God's action (Exodus 15:16b; Psalm 100:3; Isaiah 43:15; 44:2). Having delivered Israel from the miserable lot of slavery in Egypt, God made them a covenant people; and through the long and tumultuous years he educated and disciplined them in order that they might understand more deeply the meaning of their special role in history. It was Second Isaiah who understood most profoundly Israel's place in God's world-wide purpose. According to the prophet's interpretation, Israel was called to be "a light to the nations" and a Servant whose sufferings would benefit all mankind. However, in the period of Judaism, as we have seen, these spacious horizons were obscured. Jewish devotion to the Torah had the effect of sharpening the division between Jew and non-Jew and even separated Jews from their close relatives, the Samaritans (see John 4:7–30, especially verse 9, "For Jews have no dealings with Samaritans"). The last two centuries before Christ witnessed a resurgence of Jewish nationalism which led in time to the Jewish wars with Rome.[1] In A.D. 70 the Romans destroyed the Temple, leveled Jerusalem, and removed the last vestiges of Jewish statehood.

So, in the fullness of time God acted once again to reconstitute the community of Israel—no longer bound by the ethnic or nationalistic limitations of Judaism but open to all men, whether Jew or Gentile, on the basis of faith. The New Community does not establish a clean break with the People of God whose life story is portrayed in the Old Testament; rather, it is—as Paul puts it in his important discussion in Romans 9–11—"a remnant chosen by grace." It is, so to speak, a "wild olive shoot" grafted into the Olive Tree (Israel); and the "branch" is supported by the roots which reach down deeply into the biblical story of God's choice of Israel and his faithful dealings with his People (Romans 11:17–24). This whole passage deserves your thoughtful study, for it casts light upon the affinity between the Jewish and Christian communities, which cannot be effaced by differences over the Messiah.

■ The Cornerstone of the Foundation

Of the many passages in the New Testament which deal with the calling and mission of the New Com-

---

[1] The story is told in part in I Maccabees, a book which belongs to the Old Testament in expanded form (Apocrypha). For a brief, helpful discussion of the period between the Testaments, see Lawrence Toombs, *The Threshold of Christianity,* Westminster Guides to the Bible (Westminster, 1960).

munity, three have been selected for special study. You will find that each deals with an important characteristic of the Church. The first of these (I Peter 2:4–10) brings the accent down upon the truth that this Pilgrim People has been established by God's action through Jesus Christ, the "living Stone" who is the foundation of a "spiritual House." The Church is not essentially a social organization or a human institution which can be understood by sociological analysis; it is, rather, a creation of the Divine Architect who has chosen the "rejected Stone" (Jesus Christ) as the foundation. This imagery harks back to a passage in Psalm 118, a royal thanksgiving which celebrates God's gracious acts in history.[2] In this psalm (Luther's favorite) the key passage is verses 21–24, especially the jubilant cry that the Stone which the builders would have rejected as poor material has become the cornerstone of the foundation (compare Isaiah 28:16). The Stone referred to is the remnant of Israel—a "well-tested stone" with which God would carry forward his redemptive work in history. According to our passage in I Peter, the remnant is reduced to one—to Jesus Christ, the foundation of the Church. Notice that the expressions in verse 9 previously had been applied to the chosen people at the time of the making of the Covenant (see Exodus 19:4–6); now they are applied to the New Israel which was

[2] On this and related psalms see my study book, *Out of the Depths: The Psalms Speak to Us Today* (1970), chapter 4, especially pp. 82–87.

once "no people" (cf. Hosea 2:23) but which in the grace of God has become "God's people."

■ The Church in God's World-purpose

The place of the Church in the movement of God's purpose for the world, from Creation to Consummation, is developed with symphonic splendor in the Epistle to the Ephesians (Ephesians 1:1–14; 3:8–12). This epistle is such an eloquent summary of the Christian gospel in Pauline terms that it would be profitable to take a few minutes to read it through.[3] Notice that the Church is described in terms of two main images: first, the image of the temple of which Jesus Christ is the chief cornerstone (2:19–22) and, second, the distinctively Pauline image of the Body of which the Head is Christ who co-ordinates all the parts (1:22–23; 4:15–16; cf. Colossians 1:18–19).

Perhaps it would be well to concentrate your attention on the second chapter of Ephesians, where the fundamental theme of the new life and harmonious unity of the Church is sounded, a theme which is elaborated in the second part of the

[3] Some scholars believe that Ephesians is "Deutero-Pauline," that is, written by a disciple whose thinking was closely akin to Paul. The words "at Ephesus" are lacking in chapter 1, verse 1 in the best manuscripts; and the tone of the letter is quite general, without reference to local conditions at Ephesus in Asia Minor (modern Turkey). Others hold that this was a general letter which Paul intended for reading in a number of churches in Asia Minor.

epistle (chapters 4–6). Here you will want to look into the biblical meaning of the word *peace*. We usually think of peace as the absence of war; but in the Bible peace has a more positive meaning. Peace is a state of harmony, wholeness, and welfare within the community. And it is a basic biblical premise that there cannot be right relations within the community unless man is in right relation with God; for when separated from God men are at odds with themselves and with one another. The Jewish philosopher, Martin Buber, has observed:

> The true community does not arise through people's having feelings for one another (though indeed not without it), but through, first, their taking their stand in living mutual relation with the living Centre, and second, their being in living mutual relation with one another.[4]

Thus the commandment about loving God comes first, and supplies the basis for loving the neighbor (Luke 10:25–37).

As Old Testament prophets looked away from the broken and fractured society of Israel, they anticipated the coming of the age of the Messiah when the barriers of separation would be overcome and men would be brought into a new relation with God and hence with one another and even with the natural environment (Isaiah 11:1–9). Thus in Ephesians love is not a commandment but a

[4] Martin Buber, *I and Thou* (T. & T. Clark, 1937), p. 45.

new reality in human relationships which has been initiated by the prior manifestation of God's love through Jesus Christ. The most deep-seated antagonism of the time—the separating wall between Jew and Gentile—has been broken down and men are reconciled "in one body through the cross." The Church is a fellowship of love—the highest endowment of God's Spirit (see I Corinthians 13; I John 4:7–12).

■ Jesus' Prayer for the Church

The theme of the unity and fruitfulness of the Church in the world is elaborated in Jesus' so-called "High Priestly Prayer" found in John 17. Jesus has completed his mission, which is to reveal God's "name" (see Study II) to his disciples, the nucleus of the Church. In his final prayer, two prepositions are important: "out of" and "into." God has summoned a People for Christ "out of" the world (verse 6). Indeed, the New Testament word for church (*ekklesia*) literally means "called out," and suggests the conception of God calling people out of the world into a new and unique fellowship. But the Church is not taken out of the world (the secular sphere) into a sheltered and detached life; rather, it is sent "into" the world (verses 15, 18). If the Church is not *a part of* the world, it is also not *apart from* the world; rather, it is God's task force, God's mission in the world. The Church has inherited the vocation of the Servant described by Second Isaiah: to be a light to the nations and to be the instrument of God's healing the broken relationships of society.

Above all, Jesus' prayer is for the unity of the Church: "that they may be one, even as we are one" (verses 11, 22). The close relation between Christ and God in the Spirit is to be manifest in the corporate unity and harmony of the Church. And this unity is to be the most convincing demonstration to the world that Jesus has been sent by God as the Way, the Truth, and the Life.

QUESTIONS TO THINK ABOUT

1. How does Paul deal with "the mystery of Israel" in Romans 9–11? What implication does this passage have for Jewish-Christian relations today?

2. In the Bible the Church is described by various images: Flock, Vine, Building, Pilgrim People, Body, and so on. What is the intention of each of these images? Which is most meaningful for our time?

3. Does the breaking down of "the wall of separation" between Jew and Gentile have any implications for other racial and social problems facing the Church today?

4. What is the relation between the Church and the many "churches" of our time? Does the unity of the Church lie in organization? If not, what is the basis of the unity expressed in the familiar hymn, "elect from every nation, yet one o'er all the earth?"

5. What does it mean in our time for the Church to be a mission in the world? What should the Christian's attitude be toward secular expression in

art, literature, movies, folk rock, social action, and so on? On the relevance of modern literature, see, for instance, Cleanth Brooks, *The Hidden God* (Yale University Press, 1963).

Suggestions for Further Reading

Beker, J. Christiaan, *The Church Faces the World,* Westminster Guides to the Bible (Westminster, 1960). Helpful discussion of the last books of the New Testament; see especially the chapter on I Peter, "The Call to Pilgrimage," pp. 75–82.

Barrett, C. K., *A Commentary on the Epistle to the Romans,* Harper's New Testament Commentaries (Harper and Row, 1957). Excellent commentary on Paul's most important letter.

Best, Ernest, *One Body in Christ: A Study of the Relationships of the Church in the Epistles of the Apostle Paul* (S.P.C.K., 1955).

Kee, Howard, Franklin Young and Karlfried Froehlich, *Understanding the New Testament,* 2nd ed. (Prentice-Hall, 1965). See the chapters on Paul's letters and the Fourth Gospel (chapters 7–10, 14).

Minear, Paul, *Jesus and His People,* World Christian Books (Association Press, 1956); also, *Images of the Church in the New Testament* (Westminster, 1960). The latter is especially helpful for this study unit.

EPILOGUE: IN THE END

STUDY PASSAGES:

1. Revelation 21:1–8
   A New Heaven and a New
   Earth

2. Revelation 21:22 to 22:5
   The New Jerusalem

3. I Corinthians 15, especially verses
   12–23 and 51–58
   The Resurrection of the Body

4. Romans 8:18–39
   More than Conquerors

Like any drama, the biblical drama has a beginning, a climax or denouement, and an end. This
elementary observation is exceedingly important
for the understanding of the biblical view of
history. Unlike the ancient Greek historians who
believed that history moves in circles, and unlike
some modern historians who believe that the historical process is a phase of the growth and decay
of nature, the Bible affirms that our lives are part
of a great drama that moves in the direction of a
goal. The opening words of the Bible, "In the
beginning God . . ." are matched by the expecta-
tion that "in the end" God's purpose will be
realized (I Corinthians 15:24–28). All things—
history and nature, heaven and earth—are caught
up in the purpose of the God who is the First and
the Last, the Alpha and the Omega. Therefore,
telling the time is not just a chronological reckon-
ing by clocks and calendars; it is the ability to
know the content of the times (Ecclesiastes 3) and
to discern that, as a psalmist put it, our times are
in God's hand (Psalm 31:15), embraced within
his sovereign purpose.

■ The Horizons of History

It has been observed that when it comes to the
interpretation of human history there are, in general, three possible views: (1) history is meaning-
less flux from which the religious man seeks
escape (Hinduism, Buddhism); (2) history se-
cretes its own meaning in the course of cultural

evolution (Progress, Marxism); and (3) the hidden meaning of history is made known by God who, as Creator, transcends the whole finite world of sensory experience. The biblical view is that the meaning of the historical drama has its source in the Creator who comprehends the beginning and the end, who surveys and participates in the drama in its entirety, and who, according to Christian conviction, has set forth "the mystery of his will" in Jesus Christ as a "plan" which unites all things, earthly and cosmic (Ephesians 1:9–10).

In the first study unit we considered the prologue to the biblical drama of God's action in history. Now we turn our attention to the epilogue. It should be obvious that we cannot speak of either the first things or the last things except in the language of religious symbolism. In both cases we are dealing with ultimates which lie beyond the range of our finite knowledge, beyond our immediate historical experience. Therefore we must speak in the language of faith—faith which rests not upon our ability to fathom or to chart the beginning and the end, but upon the meaning that has been disclosed in the unique historical tradition beginning with the Exodus and culminating in the Christ Event. In the vision of Christian faith human history as we know it is bounded by Beginning and End, two horizons which recede into the vistas of God's eternity.[1]

[1] See further *Rediscovering the Bible,* chapter 10.

▪ Paradise Regained

A good place to begin the discussion is the portrayal of the New Heaven and the New Earth found in the last book of the New Testament, the Revelation (or Apocalypse) of Saint John the Divine. This is an exceedingly difficult book to understand because it is written in a code which cannot be deciphered without some knowledge of the persecution of the Church at the time (about A.D. 90) and the genre of literature known as "apocalyptic." [2] Much confusion has been wrought by people who have read the book as though they were gazing into a crystal ball, supposing that some mysterious blueprint for the future is hidden in it. We have tried to facilitate the study by selecting two brief passages (Revelation 21:1–8 and 21:22–22:5) in which the symbolism is not quite so obtuse. Even so, there are references which will not mean much unless you follow with a good commentary. For instance, "the Sea was no more" (21:1) is an allusion to the mythical Great Deep, the locus of rebellious powers which God has held in check since the time of Creation. [3] In other

[2] The word *apocalyptic* comes from the word *apocalypse* which means "revelation" to a seer. The best example of this type of literature in the Old Testament is the Book of Daniel, likewise written in a time of persecution (about 165 B.C.). See further my *Understanding the Old Testament,* 2nd ed. (Prentice-Hall, 1966), chapter 17.

[3] The "sea" or "chaos" imagery is discussed at length in my *Creation versus Chaos* (Association Press, 1967); see especially chapters 4 and 5.

words, this is not just the drying up of water but the overcoming of the powers of evil that menace God's creation. (Herman Melville's novel *Moby Dick* makes effective use of the biblical sea symbolism.) And the Lamb, of course, is the triumphant Christ (see John 1:29).

Two things are especially noteworthy about these passages. First, the portrayal of the New Heaven and the New Earth (cf. Isaiah 65:17–25) gathers up some of the symbols of the Paradise Story, such as the Tree of Life. Thus the end of the drama recapitulates the beginning, the New Creation corresponds to the First Creation. Secondly, the consummation of history is symbolized under the figure of the New Jerusalem, the City of God, descending from heaven. In previous studies we have found that Jerusalem in biblical tradition is more than an ordinary city. Jerusalem meant much more to the Israelite than Athens to the ancient Greek or Washington, D.C. to a present-day American. According to the "urban theology" developed in Davidic circles, Jerusalem was the City of God, the place consecrated by his presence among his people. Indeed, Jerusalem was identified with the mythical mountain of God at the center ("navel") of the earth, from which sprang a river fed by life-giving waters from the Great Deep (Psalm 46:4; Ezekiel 47:1–12). Medieval maps which pinpointed Jerusalem as the center of the universe were based on bad geography and astronomy, but they expressed an important religious conviction. To the man of faith, Jerusalem stands for the Rule of God in the midst of his People. In the Apocalypse of John we find the bold claim that history ultimately will fulfill and complete the meaning represented by Jerusalem: all nations will find their peace and unity by walking in the light of the New Jerusalem (Revelation 21:24–26; cf. Isaiah 2:14).

Thus the Bible begins with a vision of Paradise Lost and concludes with a vision of Paradise Regained. In between this prologue and epilogue unfolds the drama of God's entrance into the human struggle to win back his lost creation and to restore man to the peace, unity, and fullness of life which was intended for him. God's strategy involves the choice and discipline of a People, and finally the Way of the Cross; but the end of his redemptive activity is the final conquest of evil, death, darkness and all powers which corrupt and threaten his creation. The Church lives by this hope, and prays and strives for the coming of God's Kingdom.

■ The Decisive Battle is Won!

This brings us to the third passage, a portion of I Corinthians 15. The background of this passage is the apocalyptic view, expressed in Daniel 12:2–3 and Isaiah 26:19, of the final Consummation (the Last Judgment) when the dead will be raised up in order that the faithful may share in the conclusion of the historical drama.[4] In much of the chapter Paul argues that the "body" that will be raised is not the physical body but a *spiritual* body, surpassing the present form of our bodily existence. It is worth noting, in passing, that the body is considered to be the expression of the *person* in the wholeness of his personality, the unique self who finds life in relation to other persons and to God. Don't stumble over the literal details. Paul's intention is to affirm that the individual is *given* a future by the God who is gracious and faithful, although exactly how this is to occur, says Paul, is "a mystery" (I Corinthians 15:51). The important thing to notice in this passage is that God's victory over evil, darkness and death has already occurred—even before the End which is described pictorially in the Revelation of John as "a New Heaven and a New Earth." Of this the Christian has already been given assurance through the Resurrection of Christ, for his victory constitutes "the first fruits" which give promise that the harvest is coming (I Corinthians 15:20). Or, as Paul puts it elsewhere, through Christ's resurrection men have been given the Spirit as an "earnest"

[4] The biblical hope for a future life is not expressed in the Greek doctrine of the immortality of the soul, which presupposes a deathless element imprisoned in the body, but in the apocalyptic category of resurrection of the person. For an interpretation of the words of the Apostles' Creed, "I believe in the resurrection of the body," see Reinhold Niebuhr, *Beyond Tragedy* (Charles Scribner's Sons, 1938).

or guarantee of what is to come (II Corinthians 1:22; 5:5).

This means that the center of gravity in the Christian gospel is not a longing for a Consummation yet to come. The distinctive note of the New Testament is the announcement that the Messiah, the Christ, has already come to inaugurate his Kingdom. Already he has won the decisive victory, and therefore through him men may taste *now* the life of the New Age, "eternal life." A New Testament scholar, Oscar Cullmann, has expressed the relation between the "already" and the "not yet" in a figure of speech drawn from man's political experience. In some wars of the past the decisive battle occurred in an early stage of the campaign (for instance, the Battle of Britain during the Second World War); and though the struggle continued until the end of the war, the issue had already been decided. Cullmann uses this as an analogy to express the Christian conviction that the "earnest" of God's ultimate triumph has been given in the life, death, and resurrection of Jesus Christ, even though the historical struggle continues for an indefinite time until the outcome is evident to all.[5] In other words, the Christian gospel is a call to action in a contest whose final victory has already been won. Members of the Christian community who share this conviction live in the hope that ultimately God's Kingdom will come in fullness and that "God will

[5] Oscar Cullmann, *Christ and Time* (Westminster Press, 1950), chapter 5.

be everything to everyone" (I Corinthians 15:28).

It is significant, then, that Paul ends his discussion of the body of the resurrection not with speculation about the life beyond the grave, but with an appeal for action and responsibility (note the "therefore" of I Corinthians 15:58). There is a profound this-worldliness in the New Testament gospel, especially when it is read in the context of the whole biblical drama. The ultimate horizon of the Consummation, when all tears will be wiped away and there will be no more mourning or suffering, is intended as an endorsement of the fundamental goodness of life as we now experience it. The Christian gospel is not a utopian promise that man can achieve the good society through his own planning and efforts; nor is it the promise of release from the illusions of mortal existence, as in some Hellenistic cults of the New Testament period. Rather, it announces that none of our work is in vain because it is embraced within the purpose and love of God manifested in the midst of human history through Jesus Christ.

This is the theme to which Paul returns in the last and major letter that he wrote: the epistle to the Church at Rome (Romans 8:18–19). He looks squarely at the sufferings of the present age, the tremendous odds that are arrayed against the realization of God's purpose. He is more impressed, however, with the victory already won and the opportunity to share in the power of that victory in the present. The motive for action and responsibility is the confidence that all our human successes or failures, our joys or sorrows are embraced within the triumphant purpose of God. "In everything," writes Paul, "God works for good with those who love him." Thus, though the trials and conflicts of history are not yet concluded, the believing community lives in the assurance that "in all these things we are more than conquerors through him who loved us."

QUESTIONS TO THINK ABOUT

1. What dramatic effect is achieved in the Bible by placing the historical drama between the horizons of Beginning and End? Compare this portrayal with other views of human existence, such as the Buddhist, the humanist, the Communist, or the nihilist.

2. Is it proper to identify the Kingdom of God with the better world which men hope to achieve through social planning or revolutionary action? Is the Kingdom of God a social ideal?

3. Does it make sense to say that the New Age has already been inaugurated through the life, death, and resurrection of Jesus Christ, even before the final Consummation? What changes has this dawn of the Kingdom made in human life?

4. How does the Christian's "ultimate hope" affect or motivate his political and social responsibilities in the present historical order? What are some of the "proximate hopes" that we may expect to realize?

5. Traditionally, Christianity has preferred to express belief in the future life in terms of the resurrection of the body rather than in terms of the dualistic doctrine of the immortality (deathlessness)

of the soul. Comment on the difference between these
two ways of expression. Why is the former more
appropriate for biblical faith?

Suggestions for Further Reading

Beker, J. Christiaan, *The Church Faces the World,*
Westminster Guides to the Bible (Westminster,
1960), chapter 7. A chapter on the Revelation of
John.

Caird, G. B., *A Commentary on the Revelation of
Saint John the Divine,* Harper New Testament Commentary (Harper and Row, 1966).

Niles, D. T., *As Seeing the Invisible: A Study of
the Book of Revelation* (Harper and Row, 1961). An
illuminating study.

Minear, Paul S., *I Saw a New Earth: An Introduction to the Visions of the Apocalypse* (Corpus Books,
1968). This book will reward study.

Murdock, William R., "History and Revelation in
Jewish Apocalypticism," in *Interpretation* XXI
(1967), pp. 167–187. An important study for the
more advanced student which takes into consideration contemporary debates about the meaning of
apocaplytic literature for Christian theology.

Russell, D. S., *The Method and Message of Jewish Apocalyptic,* Old Testament Library (Westminster,
1965). A reliable survey of apocalyptic literature
from 200 B.C. to A.D. 100.

SUGGESTIONS FOR
BIBLE STUDY LEADERS

■ Purpose

Those who plan to set up a Bible Study Group should have at the outset some understanding of the uniqueness of the venture. This is not a literary circle devoted to the study of one of the great books. The uniqueness of a Bible Study Group lies in that which is at the center: the Bible. The Bible continues to exert a strange power over men's lives because it searchingly exposes the human situation in the light of God's Word spoken in the words of men, and finally made flesh in Jesus Christ. It deals with our human existence and God's involvement in it. Since all of us are inescapably involved in human existence with its glory and complexity and tragedy, there should be a place in the group for any concerned person. Those with Christian convictions (and probably they will be in the majority) will find in the Bible a deeper understanding of the relevance of biblical faith to personal life and world history. The skeptic who is sincerely seeking for light on the meaning of human existence may discover that in some respects the Bible speaks to his condition. But all members of the group will have a common purpose: to hear what the language of the Bible says to us in our life situation today.

The key word for Bible Study is *encounter*.

What takes place in the group is personal encounter with one another and with the God who speaks to us through the Bible. This distinguishes Bible Study from the kind of classroom study in which our primary relation is to a body of knowledge rather than to persons. However, the personal encounter of a Bible Study Group is not that of a glorified "bull session" in which discussion is carried on in an argumentative spirit, usually without any common frame of reference. In this case the conversation has a common center, a common frame of reference. There will be disagreements, for we each approach the Bible out of our private and cultural background, which usually means with a great deal of ignorance and even rebellion. It is the testimony of the ages, however, that God speaks to us as persons when we listen to the language of the Bible receptively, expectantly, honestly. Often this means that the presuppositions of the questions we bring to the Bible are challenged; often it means the realization that we have not asked the basic question; often it means being disturbed and changed at the very center of our being. But this is what we must expect if we risk an encounter with God.

■ Leadership

Who should be the leader? This is a difficult question. Some groups have effectively used the principle of rotation—that is, each time a different member of the group is responsible for the meeting. Often this runs against the snag that some members are not yet far enough along in their understanding of the Bible. And if the blind lead the blind, probably everyone will fall into the ditch! Other groups have found that it is better to rely on a leader who is more mature in biblical understanding (this may be a theological student, a staff leader, a professor, or a minister). No rule of thumb can be given, since groups vary so much.

Qualities of good leadership. The main task of the leader is to help the group go to the heart of the biblical passage, so that there may be a genuine encounter with the Bible rather than a mere rearranging of prejudices. This means that the leader should have some ability in group discussion and should have a fairly good knowledge of the Bible (though not necessarily that of an expert). The good leader is one who brings the discussion back to the biblical passage when it wanders astray, who patiently guides the discussion so that disagreements are fruitful, who encourages others to participate in the conversation, and who helps the group to go deeper than answers which merely scratch the surface and to avoid hasty rejection of what some may think they have outgrown. Above all, the leader is the servant of the group and should encourage the rest to have a sense of responsibility for the preparation and participation which will make the study a vital group experience.

Preparation. It cannot be emphasized too

strongly that this is a *study* group in the best sense of the word. Therefore the success of the group is dependent upon disciplined and serious preparation on the part of all members. At the minimum, this preparation must be the careful reading and pondering of the selected biblical passages with the aid of the Study Guide. This applies especially to the leader. His careful study of the material will enable him to discern what is central and what is peripheral in the group discussion. Also, he should be acquainted with the necessary background material for understanding the passages, turning whenever possible to a good commentary (see the Suggestions for Further Reading at the end of each study unit and the Selected General Bibliography).

Resource persons. Often study groups include a "resource person" (a minister, teacher, staff member) who can be consulted when information is needed on a particular point. It is important to find the kind of person who is both congenial and who will not "lord it over the group" with his contributions. Frequently, however, such knowledgeable persons tend to lean over backward on this matter—that is, they are so afraid of dominating the discussion that they do not speak until spoken to. Somehow this should be worked out so that the resource person is truly and fully a member of the group—on a level of equality with other participants rather than being set up on a pedestal because of his superior knowledge. Perhaps it would be well to forget about the idea of a resource person, and think rather of team leadership, in which a novice and an experienced person co-operate in preparing for the meeting and guiding the discussion.

■ Procedure in the Group Session

First of all, help the members of the group to feel at home with one another. In a classroom you can get by without knowing who is sitting next to you, for your concern is the mastery of a body of knowledge, not a relation between persons. Bible Study, however—as we have said—is a relation with persons by means of the spoken word, and an encounter with God who comes to men personally through his Word. Since God's Truth comes to men personally, rather than as a body of facts, the rapport of personal relationship in the group is essential.

At some point in this informal opening the leader should begin the discussion of the selected biblical passage(s). In some situations it might be appropriate to have a brief prayer or a few moments of silence. The important thing, however, is that the entire Bible Study be carried on in a serious and reverent spirit.

It should be kept in mind, above all, that Bible Study is an *interaction* between the text and the readers, between the Bible and the situation in which we find ourselves. This premise of group discussion has two interrelated aspects:

a) The primary task is to understand what the biblical writer intended to say. This may involve such questions as: Who was the author? When did he write? What was the historical and cultural setting? To whom did he write? What did he mean to say in the symbolism of language?

b) Closely related to this is the question about what the text means *for us* in our historical and cultural situation. This calls for an exercise of imagination, like that of an actor who puts himself into the script of a play. Remember that "the letter kills, it is the Spirit that gives Life." The Bible should not be treated as a soothsayer's manual which gives us literal, specific directives on everything under the sun. It may be that there are some places in the Bible where, as someone has said, God does not say anything to us except perhaps "Go, read a commentary."

Accordingly, the leader may begin by giving whatever brief background is necessary for the study of the selected biblical passage. Perhaps on subsequent occasions he could ask other members of the group to do this in order that the group as a whole may sense a shared responsibility. After this brief introduction of the historical setting of the passage, or perhaps before, it would be well to ask the group to read through the passage—or some portion of it—silently. Or it may be decided to ask someone to read the passage, or a small unit of it, aloud. If there are difficult words, they should be explained. *It is important to turn to another translation of the passage for additional light.* (See the Selected General Bibliography for translations and study aids.)

Sometimes groups have found it helpful to begin the discussion by attempting to paraphrase the passage in terms of our own modern language— that is, "put it in your own words." This is a good discipline, for it demands (1) coming to terms with what the original writer meant to say, and (2) interpreting his intention in our own categories. This may occasion the interaction between the Bible and our situation which, as we have said, is the very essence of Bible Study. Moreover, this gets away from the false idea of private interpretation of the Bible. We do not have the right to make the Bible say what we think it ought to say. We must discover what the original writer meant to say and translate that meaning into the contemporary experiences of our time. Group conversation around the Bible, guided by the Holy Spirit, will lead to a deeper understanding of biblical truth. Don't be afraid to raise "unorthodox" questions, for these may help to sharpen the issues, and God may use the skeptic to lead us into new truth. On the other hand, don't be afraid of "orthodoxy"—only try to "beat the crust back into the batter" of Christian experience. The questions included in the Study Guide at the end of each unit may help to focus the discussion.

The discussion should move according to blocks of Scripture which the leader has isolated in his private preparation. When he senses that it is time to move on, he may give a summary of a given unit of material. Above all, the leader should not be anxious about the discussion, as though its success were dependent upon his keeping it going. Don't be troubled when there are periods of silence. Don't try to hurry the group along because of the feeling that a given amount of material has to be covered; it is better to stay with a passage until you sense that the group is ready to move on. Don't answer important questions impatiently; it may be better for the group to come to the answer on its own. Or perhaps the question should be left open. As a leader, your purpose is not to lead the group to conclusions which you foresaw during your preparation; rather, let the conclusion come out of the dialectic of the discussion.

■ Closing the Session

Close on time if possible. The leader may signal the end of the discussion by giving a brief summary, and showing the relation of the discussion to the previous study session or to studies that follow. It may be appropriate to follow the summary with a brief prayer, such as the words found in Psalm 139:23–24.

Keep in mind that the foregoing remarks are only suggestions. No plan should be superimposed inflexibly upon a Bible Study Group.

SELECTED GENERAL BIBLIOGRAPHY

BIBLE TRANSLATIONS

(When studying the English Bible it is important to consult more than one translation.)

The Revised Standard Version of the Bible and the Apocrypha (Division of Christian Education, National Council of Churches, 1946 and 1952). A reliable, widely used translation which retains, wherever possible, readings of the Authorized (King James) Version.

The Torah: The Five Books of Moses (Jewish Publication Society of America, 1962). Translation of the Pentateuch by Jewish scholars.

The New Testament in Modern English, translated by J. B. Phillips (Macmillan, 1963). A free translation by a British scholar. Portions of the Old Testament are now available.

Good News for Modern Man: The New Testament in Today's English Version, translated by R. G. Bratcher (American Bible Society, 1966). A lively translation into vernacular English. Portions of the Old Testament are also available.

The Jerusalem Bible (see below under STUDY AIDS).

The New English Bible (Oxford Press, Cambridge University Press, 1970). A fresh, idiomatic translation by a team of British scholars. (See also the fresh translations given in the Anchor Bible, listed below.)

STUDY AIDS

The Oxford Annotated Bible with the Apocrypha, edited by Herbert G. May and Bruce M. Metzger

(Oxford, 1965). A valuable work, based on the Revised Standard Version and provided with brief articles, notes to the text, maps, and other aids.

The Jerusalem Bible, edited by Alexander Jones (Doubleday, 1966). A reliable translation from the original languages by Roman Catholic scholars; provided with introductory articles, annotations, and other study aids.

Westminster Study Edition of the Holy Bible (Westminster Press, 1948). Based on the Authorized (King James) Version, this also contains excellent introductory articles, annotations to the text, and other helpful study aids.

The Interpreter's Dictionary of the Bible, in 4 volumes, edited by G. A. Buttrick and others (Abingdon, 1962). An excellent dictionary for following up particular points.

The Westminster Historical Atlas to the Bible, rev. ed., edited by G. Ernest Wright and Floyd V. Filson (Westminster, 1956). One of several excellent atlases now available; highly recommended for accuracy of discussion and cartography.

COMMENTARY SETS

(Specific commentaries on biblical books are mentioned in the Suggestions for Further Reading at the end of each study unit.)

The Interpreter's Bible, edited by G. A. Buttrick and others (Abingdon, 1952–57).

The Jerome Biblical Commentary, edited by Raymond E. Brown and others (Prentice-Hall, 1968). A very good commentary in one volume by Roman Catholic scholars.

The Old Testament Library, edited by G. Ernest Wright and others (Westminster, 1962 and on).

A number of important commentaries have appeared in this series.

Peake's Commentary on the Bible, revised edition, edited by Matthew Black and H. H. Rowley (Nelson, 1962). A standard one-volume commentary updated.

The Layman's Bible Commentary, in 25 volumes, edited by Balmer Kelly (John Knox, 1959). Concise and readable.

The Torch Bible Commentaries, in 39 volumes, edited by John Marsh and Alan Richardson (SCM Press, 1952 and on). A valuable, nontechnical series.

The Anchor Bible, edited by W. F. Albright and D. N. Freedman (Doubleday, 1964 and on). Fresh translations of the biblical books with introduction and annotations.

GENERAL WORKS

(Works dealing with specific topics are listed in the Suggestions for Further Reading at the end of each study unit or in footnotes along the way.)

ANDERSON, BERNHARD W., *Rediscovering the Bible* (Association Press, 1951). Presents in fuller detail the general approach that is followed in this Study Guide. Later developments in biblical studies are reflected in *Understanding the Old Testament,* 2nd ed. (Prentice-Hall, 1966)—a widely used text which interweaves history, literature, and theology of the Old Testament. Also *Creation versus Chaos* (Association Press, 1967), a study of creation and related matters against the background of ancient religions.

DE DIETRICH, SUZANNE, *God's Unfolding Purpose: A Guide to the Study of the Bible,* translated from the French by Robert McAfee Brown (Westminster, 1960). A valuable, devotional book which is recommended to supplement this Bible Study.

KEE, HOWARD, FRANKLIN YOUNG and KARLFRIED FROEHLICH, *Understanding the New Testament,* 2nd ed. (Prentice-Hall, 1965). A companion to *Understanding the Old Testament,* listed above. A third edition of both these volumes is now in preparation.

WESTERMANN, CLAUS, *A Thousand Years and a Day: Our Times in the Old Testament* (Fortress Press, 1962). Sets forth the view that the thousand years of Old Testament tradition find their climax in "the day" of Christ's coming. The companion book by Gerhard Gloege, *The Day of His Coming: Our Times in the New Testament* (Fortress Press, 1967) focuses on the Day of Christ's coming in the context of the thousand years of Old Testament tradition.

WESTERMANN, CLAUS, *Our Controversial Bible* (Augsburg Publishng House, 1969). Based on a series of radio lectures. Translator Darold H. Beekmann has provided a good bibliographical guide to books that have appeared in the last decade.